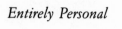

Entirely Personal

ENTIRELY PERSONAL

by
PAUL GREENBERG

UNIVERSITY PRESS OF MISSISSIPPI
Jackson | *London*

Library of Congress Cataloging-in-Publication Data

Greenberg, Paul, 1937–
    Entirely personal / by Paul Greenberg.
        p.   cm.
    ISBN 0-87805-551-7 (alk. paper)
    1. Greenberg, Paul, 1937– . 2. Journalists—United States—
Biography. 3. United States—History—20th century. 4. United
States—Social conditions—20th century. I. Title.
PN4874.3678A3   1992
814′.54—dc20   91-32348
                                                                       CIP

British Library Cataloging-in-Publication data available

To Ben And Sarah Greenberg

And the memory of my childhood

Contents

VI | THE NATION

VII | BASEBALL AS METAPHOR

Acknowledgments

Books begin as great ideas and become great chores. My thanks to JoAnne Prichard, senior editor of the University Press of Mississippi, who came up with the idea and kept it from becoming a chore. She not only initiated *Entirely Personal* but saw it to completion with businesslike grace.

I am indebted to the University Press for allowing me to revisit some of my more personal essays, rework them, and send them out into the world in new bindings. For a writer, it's like having a chance to relive one's words, exorcising a wayward spirit here and inserting what one hopes will be a better one there. It is a rare thing, a chance to edit one's past.

Almost all these essays originally appeared in the *Pine Bluff Commercial*, which has tolerated me for some three decades now. Just as the people of Pine Bluff have. Many of these selections were distributed by the Los Angeles Times Syndicate, whose editors I have come to rely upon.

Carolyn Greenberg, who edited and distributed my newspaper column for years as a one-woman syndicate, helped copyread these essays with her expert, experienced, and loving eye. And various of these pieces took shape one way or another through stimulating discussions over the years with E. W. Freeman III, a former publisher of the *Commercial*.

I am grateful to all.

Introduction

Why do people read political columns?

Maybe for the same reasons they read the comic strips: entertainment, enlightenment, provocation, and validation. And surely for one more reason. It's the same reason many of us don't want to die. We want to see what happens next—and hear what is said about it. What is event without reaction, text without commentary?

In the course of following the commentary, we develop an interest in the commentator—whether it's William F. Buckley, Gabriel Heatter, Saint Augustine, "The Far Side's" Gary Larson .... Sometimes we read not to find out what's in the news but what's in the commentator. The fortunate columnist establishes a personal relationship with the reader. It's a kind of one-way intimacy. To write is to risk exposure; few things are so revealing as words.

Just like a normal human being, the writer may be the sum of all that he has met, beginning with family. Which is how this book begins. No one can read many of the pieces in this collection without sensing the presence of the immigrant generation and the immigrant experience in America during the first part of this century. That presence is very much with me: a mother who survived war and poverty in Europe, who always feared and detested both but was not bowed by either. A short woman, Sarah Greenberg never slumped.

My father, complete with Yiddish accent, remains the most American figure I've ever known—optimistic, resilient, the eternal entrepreneur on however modest a scale, charming and convinced of his charm, a merchant who knew that any firm's most valuable asset is its good will. He believed in repeat business in every sphere—in the crown of a good name.

I come from a matriarchal family traceable on these shores to my paternal grandmother, Bubba Chava. She was the one who brought over my mother to marry my father in 1921. Her name means Eve, appropriately enough, and she was as tough as my grandfather Chaim was gentle. The women in my family always struck me as knowing what was important in life—family, children, continuity—and the men as needing to be taught. Maybe that's why I was never able to get into feminism beyond women's suffrage and equal-pay-for-equal-work. The women I grew up with seemed more than capable of taking care of themselves.

The nascent men's movement is an even greater mystery to me, perhaps because I had a father who was a father. By example rather than precept (expressing sentiment openly made him uneasy) he made it clear that the two most important things in life were prayer, in which he could pour out all his emotions, and work. He had a talent for both. Ben Greenberg changed businesses from time to time but stayed at the same location. He liked making money but I don't think he was ever as happy or as proud of his work as when he was fixing shoes. I noticed he would never let a sloppy job out of the store. He was miserable as a pawnbroker, and he was less so selling furniture on credit.

Without ever being told explicitly, which was not done in my family, I came to understand that the most important consideration in society was not the role of women or of men but their union: the family. The emphasis was on the children, the representatives of the future. Very American. Very Jewish.

Someone once asked me how much of my writing was influenced by my being Jewish. The immediate, spontaneous response that formed in my mind was: "Every word, including *and* and *the*." The longest section in this collection is the one on religion. I remember a friend telling me in college that if I weren't Jewish, "you'd just dry up." I think she had it right.

Coming up in a traditional Jewish family in a Southern town during the Forties and Fifties meant being completely apart and completely together—completely apart from the larger world and completely together in one's self. As one grew older, the child's world expanded and faded into the larger one. Then one could be as whole as everyone else and just as confused. This is called maturity. Maybe things are never as clear as in one's childhood.

My fear and suspicion of the bubble Popularity may date from those early years in Shreveport, when to have been in the vast majority would have meant betraying one's identity. I've always felt uneasy when taking some position I knew would be popular, and never more comfortable and secure than when in the minority, preferably a minority of one. My boss at the old *Chicago Daily News* once applied the adjective "perverse" to my views during the course of a heated editorial conference, and I felt strangely comforted. It's being in the mainstream that makes me nervous. Maybe it was being exposed to the Prophets too early—they were forever denouncing the complacent majority—but I suspect it has a lot to do with growing up Jewish in Shreveport, Louisiana.

The South, particularly the small-town South, was simply the world as I was growing up in Shreveport. I would no more have taken note of being Southern in my early years than a fish might have noticed the water. The South was just there. Only when I would leave, and the South disappear, would I notice and begin to think on what the South is, or was, usually in response to that inevitable, unanswerable, irresistible and tiresome question: "What is the South really like?"

Other themes recur in these pieces: an interest in history that amounts almost to historicism; a reverence for language, for words as holy vessels; and a wish that values like freedom and justice could be combined with peace—an ordered liberty, as the founding fathers might say. One need not be a great scholar of the Jewish past to see where such themes come from. I call myself an "ideologically unreliable conservative," but I also fancy a description applied to one of my many heroes, Edmund Burke—"a liberal counter-revolutionary." One more theme seems to occur with increasing frequency as I grow older: a hunger and thirst for the presence of God, a want that may be a natural part of the aging process, and is as insistent as an adolescent's sex drive.

Influences glare out of these pieces like so many spotlights. Books, books, and books, beginning and ending with the Bible. There is George Orwell, the first writer I ever read who made politics more than a theoretical game or spectator sport—who connected it with the way one lives. He remains a model for commentators who would like to enter into the texture of their readers' lives. José Ortega y Gasset and Learned Hand and Daniel Boorstin and Flannery O'Connor and Walker Percy—each encountered at different times, some held onto, others let go.

Being raised on Donald Ewing's editorials in the *Shreveport Times* has had its effect. Every now and then a strange right-wing idea will rise like some phoenix in my mind, and I don't have to wonder where it came from. One reason I've enjoyed being an editorial writer in a small town is that few other jobs allow one to shape the mentality of a whole generation of readers coming of age. It's not the individual endorsements or political stands that make editorials influential but the day-by-day, week-by-week, year-by-year shaping of attitudes. Depending on their quality, editorials can be an education or a variant of the Chinese water torture. Surely my younger readers will someday be as appalled as I am at the notions that can be picked up from reading editorials regularly in one's formative years, and by how they may refuse to go away but take up lodgings in some cobwebbed corner of the mind, reappearing at odd hours.

What experiences shaped these commentaries? Well, I was a fan of small towns long before going to study history at Columbia University in New York City, an experience that confirmed my most cherished prejudices about big cities, parochial minds, and academic prose. Failing the oral examination for the Ph.D.—not once but twice— leaves you impervious to any political or professional rejection in the future; you've already been through that.

On returning to Columbia years later to judge the Pulitzer entries, I looked up the room in Fayerweather Hall where I had taken the orals for the second time. How narrow it was. I tried to find the room in Hamilton where I had taken them the first, equally disastrous time, but was unable to. Maybe they had remodeled the building, or I my memory. Anyway, I did not come out of those rooms with empty hands, much as I thought so at the time. The rejection has become a source of strength, even pride. For years I didn't mention that double failure; now I notice that I can hardly wait to introduce it into a conversation. I'm not sure which attitude is worse.

I do not seem to thrive above a certain degree of latitude. I spent a year to the day as an editorial writer at the late *Chicago Daily News,* watching a once great newspaper slide into mediocrity as it tried to replace quality with popularity, achieving neither. Then I lit out for the territories again. Fortunately, my old boss at the *Pine Bluff Commercial*—Ed Freeman—was willing to take me back. My tendency to celebrate small-town life and be leery of large and prestigious organizations may be related to my own experiences.

Originally, the pieces on baseball in this section had been scattered discreetly among the more "serious" essays, till it dawned on me that they merited a section of their own. It's called "Baseball as Metaphor," but maybe some of the other sections should be presented as metaphors about baseball, so central and lovely is this always restorative game in my entirely personal universe. It's certainly more serious than a lot of political commentary.

I grew up on David Lawrence, George Sokolsky, and Westbrook Pegler in the old *Shreveport Times*—and then graduated to Max Lerner and Murray Kempton in the old *New York Post.* Students at Columbia in the blissful Fifties bought the *New York Times* for the news and the *Post* for the columnists—just as we went to Chock Full o' Nuts for coffee and the Good Humor Man for ice cream on a stick.

What did the columnists provide that so attracted us? Or rather, what did we hope they would provide when we turned to the editorial section with a rustle of pages and hope? The same things readers must look for now: Insight. Contact with the way life is lived. And continuity. We used the columnists and our reactions to them as benchmarks of our own changes, much as Binx Bolling in Walker

Percy's *The Moviegoer* went to old movies to gauge how much he had developed, or deteriorated, since the last time he had seen the same film. To serve such a purpose, the columnists had to be regulars; we had to read their poorest as well as best pieces, and get to know their moods to predict how they would react to the news of the day. That was half the fun. It was delightful when they surprised us. It was assuring when they didn't; Walter Lippmann was in his semi-detached heaven and all was right with the world.

The time when no event, trend or idea was complete before it was reviewed by the magisterial Lippmann passed some time in the Sixties. Joe Kraft, who spent a prodigious career being billed as the next Lippmann, never made it—not because of anything he wrote or didn't write, but because the times didn't call for another Lippmann, another elevated art critic of American politics. The job category known as Lippmann simply ceased to be. The market demanded a newer, different, more personal kind of commentary—a sports model. (The auto industry faces much the same challenge from time to time.) Result: a new crop of columnists supplanted the old sages.

Phil Geyelin, who used to write a column for the *Washington Post*, told me years ago that the political column was a dying art form. You would never know it from the proliferating number of columnists in American newspapers. At this juncture, it may be the American *editorial* that is dying and needs resuscitation. It's a sad and curious lapse in a country that once produced editorial writers like William Allen White, Grover C. Hall Jr., and Henry Watterson. Now columnists rush to fill the vacuum of opinion left by the decline of the editorial.

What is killing the great American editorial? My theory is that its slow demise can be traced to the baneful effects of the editorial conference that begins the day at so many American dailies. Ideas that originate in one mind are soon whittled down to fit the ideological preferences and cautious instincts of everybody around the table. By the end of the hour, anything distinctive may be lost in the shavings. Do you know any painter or sculptor or author who would invite a roomful of colleagues to talk over his idea for a work of art before beginning it? The standard American editorial tends to read like a committee report because it is. Anything personal or different is stifled at birth. Happily, there are exceptions to this drab rule, but they remain all too few. Such is the work of the collective mentality.

The great mystery about the editorial-as-soporific is why anyone would write like that. Surely it takes more time and effort to turn out a thoroughly insipid editorial than to commit lively commentary. Even outrageous, atrocious, dead-wrong rhetoric interests me more than the kind of opinion that is so balanced and safe and mediocre that in the end it lacks opinion. Yet the country is awash in attempts to write editorials that don't much editorialize.

The result has been a demand for the personal in opinion writing. By personal columns, I don't mean pieces about one's spouse, children, or dog in roughly that ascending order of interest to others. I mean opinion about issues or events that involve all of us, yet can be seen through the filter of one writer's personal sensibility. As the editorial has faded, the column has prospered.

The unexamined assumption that the tension in political commentary lies between writer and subject excludes a third and necessary partner in this complex transaction: the reader. In order for the exchange to be complete, the writer must risk exposure and the reader judgment. Writing-and-reading are only different aspects of one participant sport—just as listening and talking are both part of the best conversation.

It's easier to explain why people read syndicated columns than why people write them. I am slowly coming to believe it's a masochistic form of ego gratification, a subspecies of what the psychiatrists call "writing behavior." Writing a syndicated column, like playing third base or leading a symphony orchestra, is one of those activities that may look easier than it is. One of the constants of an editor's mail is the flow of proposals from folks who want to write columns on a regular basis. Preachers and college professors seem particularly susceptible to the virus. My first word of advice about such an undertaking is simple—Don't! But I know they won't take it. If I didn't listen to such sensible counsel, why should they? There is something irresistible about columnizing—like sliding down a banister. How else can you make a fool of yourself in front of so many people? Besides, how does a fellow know what he really thinks about a subject until he writes it out?

I consider myself a word man, yet in choosing the more personal of my columns for this book, I was struck by how often the same visual images recur in different contexts: bugs splattering against the windshield of an old Chevy speeding down a two-lane highway on a dark summer night in bayou country; the Edward Hopper light of Main Streets in small towns; an empty beach; faded pictures in family albums; the lesser rituals of family, faith, and friendship; the feel of ballparks, mostly minor-league; and the interiors of coffee shops, bookstores, newsrooms and shoe shops that no longer exist except in the most affective and creative of realms, that of memory. Sights and sounds and smells unlock the words. Revising these recollections, I realize—like Jacob—that these places were holy and I did not know it.

The current, misplaced emphasis on the technique of writing rather than on images and ideas may be the surest sign of the malaise that besets much of American opinionating. It was Raymond Carver who warned that, when a writer starts talking about technique, you know he's out of ideas. The columnist gets to aim for a work of art every time. That's what makes writing, like baseball, such a promising and heartbreaking venture.

Archy the Cockroach, who used to come out at night to ghostwrite Don Marquis's column in the old *New York Sun* circa 1916, had it right:

> boss i am disappointed in
> some of your readers they
> are always asking how does
> archy work the shift so as to get a
> new line or how does archy do
> this or do that they
> are always interested in technical

details when the main question is
whether the stuff is
literature or not

Paul Greenberg
Pine Bluff, Arkansas

January 21, 1992

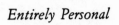
Entirely Personal

1 | ON FAMILY

America for Sale

I wonder what Sarah Greenberg would think about the latest twist to immigration laws. It would allow people to enter the United States if they have $2 million to invest and can employ ten people.

Sarah Greenberg didn't have $2 million when she got to the Port of Boston on February 10, 1921. She was nineteen-year-old Sarah Ackerman then, and I wasn't even a twinkle in her eye. She did have a certain knowledge of the immigration laws, gained standing in line for days around the American Embassy in Warsaw. She would remember almost wearing out the rubber heels on her shoes. She used them as erasers to change the answers on her visa application every time a new rumor would make it down the line to her—the United States was letting in only skilled labor, only unskilled labor, only people 21 years or older, only people under 21...

Somehow she made it, as somehow she had made it through the chaos of the First World War. For the rest of her life, she would never waste anything. I grew up in a house in which the handkerchiefs were mended, in which old washcloths and dustrags were sewn together to make one good one. A country girl from the village of Mordt in eastern Poland, she was a daughter of the miller, Paesach the Gritsmaker, for whom I would be named. I have a picture of him in skullcap and beard. He didn't have $2 million, either, though he was considered a substantial citizen for a time. His labor force consisted of a horse, and when the horse was sick my grandfather would hitch himself up and turn the grinding stone.

The war, the First World War, ended all that. My grandfather didn't survive it; my mother would wake up as a young girl and not know whether the Germans or the Russians were occupying the town that day. She much preferred the Germans, on at least two counts: There were often Jewish boys among the German soldiers (this was the *First World War*) and, when the Germans took whatever little food the family had, they paid for it with scrip, unlike the Russians. The scrip was worthless, of course, but my mother was one who always appreciated a gesture.

The war never left her. Fifty years later, murmuring in her last illness, she would keep telling her youngest child: "That's Bubba Rosa and me, that's Bubba Rosa and me..." I thought it was just the sedatives making her ramble, bringing back memories of my grandmother. Then I noticed the television set high up in the corner of the hospital room. On the screen were pictures of another war, this one in Vietnam, and there was a woman wandering on some godforsaken road, abandoned, confused, holding the hand of her child as troops moved past and artillery rounds exploded in the distance. "That's Bubba Rosa and me," my mother was telling me. Across time and continents, the horror and stupidity of war had not changed.

All my mother wanted of Poland was out. In our house, when someone made any remark that might be construed as even vaguely critical of the economy or the political system or anything American, she would say nothing. And her silence would fill the room like a shriek. She would give the speaker what we kids called The Look. It was an expression of contempt deeper than any words. The message was clear enough: What do you know of persecution, desperation, hunger, want, who only America know? My mother pronounced the word "Europe" like a curse.

So I wonder what she would think about the proposal to put people with $2 million ahead of everybody else waiting to get into this country. I wonder what she would think of the idea that American citizenship could be bought, and of some of the people who would rush to buy it—deposed dictators, drug kings, the type who think everything's for sale, including America. This $2 million provision is for the Ferdinand Marcoses of the world, not the Sarah Ackermans. I don't think she would say anything about it, but I can see The Look now.

Growing Up in Shreveport

I suspect there were as many ways of growing up Jewish in Shreveport during the 1940s and 1950s as there were Jews. But in the interest of brevity, those ways can be narrowed down to two—Orthodox and Reform, which roughly coincide with East European Jewish and German Jewish.

In my youngest years I thought of "the Reform" as another Christian sect—or anyway, a breed apart. To do justice to the subject, this memoir would have to be balanced by someone who grew up on the other side of the aisle.

I have come across various sociologists since who have tried to explain the mutual wariness between Reform and Orthodox; they tend to focus on the Reform Jews' fears of too close an association with Jews of a later immigration, and how that might affect their own hard-won, Americanized status. Less attention is paid to the fears Reform Jews aroused in us—that of losing our roots and distinctiveness, of blending into the homogeneous crowd.

The two groups largely have melded by now in these latitudes and much has been gained; the distinctions were essentially social and cultural rather than having anything to do with the essence of things.

Perhaps something has been lost, too. I belong to a Reform

congregation in Pine Bluff now—it's the only Jewish congregation in town—and occasionally older members of the temple will look back nostalgically to a time when services were "more understandable" and more "spiritual."

My nostalgia has a different focus. A Reform Jew now, I have about despaired of ever learning two honest, simple things my father seemed to know instinctively. One was how to fix a pair of shoes, the other how to pray with all one's might—with *kavanah*. With *intention*.

There seemed two worlds back then, the Jewish and the outside world, the worlds of home and street, Hebrew School and public school, Jewish holidays and everybody else's. There were two languages (Yiddish and English), two diets (kosher and *trefe*) and two whole sets of appropriate behavior that might have confused an adult but that a child learns as naturally as he does two languages.

My grandmother, who left Europe just in time, would take care of me while my parents worked; she could have arrived not from another continent but from another time.

Bubba Rosa might have just stepped out of the Middle Ages, with her stories of imps and devils, and her mixture of piety and superstition (now called folklore in this more ethnic-conscious age). Then I would go to school to learn math, science, English, social studies. They seemed to me two separate but equally mythical explanations of the world, each useful in a different environment.

Early on I remember taking long walks on Saturday to visit my grandmother's friends (it is forbidden to ride on the Sabbath) and waiting for three stars to come out that night to turn on the lights and radio (it is forbidden to kindle fire on the Sabbath).

The Orthodox Jewish community might have been a small Jewish village—a *shtetel*—replanted from Eastern Europe, or maybe from the set of "Fiddler on the Roof." It had its leaders and followers, its characters and mainstays, its petty feuds and jealousies that disappeared when there was something that touched all, like the terrible news from Europe, or word of the Jewish state being created in Palestine.

There always seemed to be a lot of visitors around, which made life exciting for a youngster. During the war years, on Jewish holidays and many a weekend, the house was full to overflowing with Jewish boys from Barksdale Air Force Base—which was understandable, there being an eligible daughter in the household.

My older sister would marry one of them in a home ceremony that I can remember vividly. She would move to New York, but she can't seem to stay away from Shreveport for very long, and her eyes still light up when she talks about old friends and old times. She still keeps an apartment in Shreveport, a *pied-a-terre* in her youth.

As the years passed, the Jewish world grew smaller and smaller, and the other larger and larger, encompassing it. Or perhaps the two worlds and their common values only grew together. Old-timers passed on and traditions faded. But a powerful bond remained: the memory of that small world, its closeness, warmth, shared values— and the lessons it had to teach.

Four afternoons a week, I would leave Creswell Elementary School and walk through Columbia Park to take the trolley down Line Avenue to Agudath Achim Synagogue. I remember talking with other oh-so-serious youngsters about how we weren't learning anything important in Hebrew School. Now, year by year, everything else seems to dwindle in importance compared to what Rabbi Leo Brener taught there.

It's clear now, looking back, where the center of moral gravity was for Shreveport's Orthodox Jews, and that was in the deliberate, unobtrusive style of Rabbi Brener—just Rabbi to most of us. I must have been half grown before I realized he had a name as well as a title.

At the time, his standards and style seemed at variance with what that other world was stressing, and with what much of the Jewish world valued, too—upward mobility, material success, bigger and better.... His ways seemed so simple, so plain, that no child might have thought of him as capital-I important. But there were hints—in the way he deliberated before answering almost any question of consequence, as if life and the way it was lived was the most important thing, and in a certain formality of manner that never kept him from making corny jokes.

I can remember listening to Rabbi Brener's monthly sermon in Yiddish, a practice that faded away with Yiddish speakers in the congregation, and trying in my mind to translate it simultaneously, the way I'd heard they did at the United Nations.

I might have been able to get the words right but not the spirit. It was the spirit of simple, plain, unadorned discourse on the sublime. The combination may explain why a lot of us grew up to admire Rabbi, and to feel his presence long after we left Shreveport.

One felt most Jewish, most distinctive, in the other world, that of public school. This being the Bible Belt, Jews were expected/assumed to know the Bible as a kind of inside story. I remember friends asking if we still sacrificed animals, and what Moses was really like, and how we celebrated Christmas, and feeling I had better know the right answers or else I would let the team down.

No one had to say some things out loud; it was understood that Jewish kids were supposed to study hard, keep out of trouble and know the Bible. The Jews I've met from big cities in the North with their Jewish neighborhoods the size of whole cities don't know what I'm talking about but Southern Jews, especially those from small towns, do.

There were occasional awkward times, too. Like at Christmas when everybody was supposed to sing carols. I remember mouthing a lot of words, then chiming in on those I figured would be OK. ("Born is the King of I-I-srael.") It was a compromise between the demands of faith and sociability.

I think Thanksgiving is still my favorite holiday because *everybody* could celebrate it with a clear conscience.

Then there were the religious revivals (Christians only) that swept through the schools now and then. There was that awful day the Gideons came distributing New Testaments. I was unable to resist—I still can't turn down any book—and felt as if I'd sold out. I wouldn't read a New Testament until years later, when there was nothing else around in the Army. Doggone if it didn't turn out to be a very Jewish book—though with a wondrously different arrangement of the familiar verses from the Hebrew Bible.

Being Jewish also gave one a certain fellow feeling for other distinctive minorities—Greek and Syrian kids, for example—as if we all belonged to a secret society. Being an outsider has its advantages, too. It lends perspective.

Growing up Jewish in Shreveport may not have been that different from growing up anything else, but it seemed so at the time. It was a bit like having a very large extended family with its own distinctive ways that, however natural they seemed to you, struck others as exotic, mysterious, fascinating. For no special reason, one really felt rather special.

Family Feud

The organizers of the Governor's Conference on Families at Pine Bluff got themselves out-organized.

It was clear enough from the program how the show was supposed to go, and what conclusions the cast was supposed to reach: On the first day, one social scientist reviewed all the benefits European governments were handing out to families—with the unavoidable implication that this country ought to go and do likewise. That evening, a statistician explained how the traditional family model was fading and how, if government concentrated on aiding the very young and very old, the family could take care of itself. Next day, a distinguished physician explained that she was a middle-roader at this conference. The twofold burden of her middle-of-the-road speech was that (1) government needed to support families, and (2) if it didn't, it must extend help directly to children. The title of her address: "Protecting the Family from Itself."

According to the script, the conferees, having thus been educated, would go on to pass a series of resolutions urging more or different government aid programs. Messy questions like abortion, sex education, and the inculcation of moral values would be neatly sidestepped and the conference would put its seal of approval on a list of new government programs.

There was to be no dangerous wandering away from the preordained political track, even if the conference also featured an election for delegates to the coming national conference on families. According to the conference coordinator, the participants had been told "that there could be no campaigning in the way of flyers, handouts or posters..." That kind of decree rings a warning bell in any newspaperman's mind. This was clearly not a conference on the First Amendment.

Telling Americans not to politick, or at least to keep it to a minimum, had the usual result. Politics overflowed into everything, demonstrating that not just those on a government payroll can stack a conference. Indeed, when it comes to social discipline and political organization, the organizers down from Washington or Little Rock could have taken some lessons from the militants who showed up with their own agenda and their own candidates—and busloads of votes to put them across. The people mobilized by FLAG (Family, Life, America and God) seemed to want to talk about all the subjects the conference's leadership didn't. They apparently didn't need any lectures about the breakdown of the traditional family in America; they seemed aware of it even before they stepped off the buses and went directly to vote. But what others presented as the solution—government intervention—they called the problem.

The vocabularies of the two sides could not have been more different. While one side dispensed the latest in sociobabble, the other thundered back in capital letters about the prevalence of SIN and CORRUPTION in American Life. And these folks were not going to be put off by nice people conducting breathing exercises in the workshops. They piled off the church buses and chartered specials like whole casts out of a Flannery O'Connor novel, armed with votes and out to crush the threats they perceived against home, family, and church. Their mentality was summed up by a young doctor who serves on the advisory board of FLAG. He claimed that whatever his people had wanted to discuss had been dismissed as "not a germane topic." He wanted to talk of the Spiritual Decline of America, made manifest to him in The Media. The philosophy of the conference, he felt, "differs from the heartbeat of most Americans." He confided that ideally the best form of government would be a theocracy, like that of Moses in the Old Testament, though unfortunately that was no longer practical.

FLAG had done an impressive job of organizing those who feel much put upon by an intrusive and increasingly alien society. Yet how quickly the defenders became aggressors. It proved a small step from talking about the need to preserve spiritual values in the home to thrusting prayer back into the public schools. Those who railed against the dangers of governmental control were soon considering ways to control the decadent Media. To offset government interference, that handiest of weapons was being trundled out—government interference.

It was not enough to defend private values within home and church; those values were to be imposed on others as well. (The young doctor's attachment to theocracy might not be entirely abstract.) It was this contradictory desire to preserve their private values and control the public arena, too, that gave these FLAG wavers the strange air of a group of aggressive Amish, if that can be imagined. At the heart of their striking social organization and political discipline lay a confession of weakness, as if they were saying that private values could not survive without the approval and support of the state. What these defenders of the faith seemed to lack most was faith.

The sophisticates' response to this wave of reaction was a disdain slightly diluted with fear and loathing. One recalls how Andrew Sarris reviewed *Wise Blood,* the movie version of a Flannery O'Connor story: "I think every thoughtful person should see *Wise Blood* once, if only to experience a profound and original depression. I am not sure that Flannery O'Connor's vivid gargoyles belong on a movie screen. When one actually sees them in the flesh they seem too desperately disconnected for the black humor of their colorful dialogue to redeem them. I don't want to keep falling back on Aristotle's very sketchy notations on the subject but the lower depths have always seemed a very dangerous starting point for any sort of dramatic development..." Evidently Mr. Sarris is unaware that Flannery O'Connor wrote theology, not just comedy, though the two may be inextricably mixed, given the human condition. The official tone of the conference betrayed much the same unawareness of what made these people tick—and the same unrelenting condescension for the lower orders.

The innocents put in charge of some of the workshops where FLAG concentrated its power soon realized that they were attempting to restrain a machine that would have made Mayor Daley's look a little short on discipline. There was no stopping these people from jumping the track. "They got off on the morality issues," as one moderator observed. Instead of day care and Flextime, they proceeded to raise issues like these: "In what ways can we lessen the control of the federal government and give more to the local authorities? In what ways can sex education, if taught, be supportive of parents' values and morals? How can we instill in today's youth a respect for and understanding of American heritage and patriotism?" Not precisely what the conference's organizers had in mind.

It was not very assuring to walk into one of these sessions, hear a resolution urging that all homosexuals be purged from the schools, and then see nine out of ten hands shoot up in immediate approval, as though they were being pulled by a single invisible cord. No discussion. No talk of family, fairness or conscience, or of scientific inquiry or what is humane and reasonable, but just the vote and the struggle for dominance. Ignorance in action is a frightening spectacle—as frightening as a small group deciding what subjects Americans may or may not discuss.

In the end, the conference's organizers and those who insisted on organizing themselves passed each other like ships in the night, one with cannons blazing and FLAG flying, the other equipped mainly with disdain, unable to acknowledge that it was trying to put over a social and political agenda of its own. The two sides in this slugging match offered a striking contrast in style and manner, but in one way they were very much alike—in their intolerance for one another. As for the American family, it was as ignored as ever in all the political skirmishing. After all, there was a fight to be won or lost here.

If the White House Conference on Families is anything like the conference in Pine Bluff, it should be the greatest show since the Scopes Trial, exposing the depth of cultural divisions in American society and almost nothing of the forces that hold it together, like the American family.

On one side will be those so convinced of their enlightenment that issues other than their own will be dismissed as Single Issues. To quote the national conference's chairperson, Jim Guy Tucker: "We have to get through the minefield of single-issue views." One of the conference's publicity people, Anna Bedford, put it this way: "I'm afraid that many churches are getting behind issues they feel strongly about. And I'm afraid that can sidetrack the real issues that concern families."

A real issue, one gathered from Mrs. Bedford, is the need to confront the problems of the family through a "corporate orientation." To back up that view, she cited the gospel from Kenneth Keniston's book, *All Our Children:* "We Americans like to see ourselves as a child-loving society. But in fact...we care about our children as we do our real estate—we love it a whole lot if it's ours, but if it's somebody else's we can tolerate a lot of pain and damage, we don't really concern ourselves..."

This is the kind of half-truth that infuriates those who believe in the other half. It occurs to them soon enough that children who are said to belong to everyone may belong to no one, and that corporate responsibility for child rearing may produce as much individualism as corporate secretarial pools. After all, not before now has being a ward of the state or of some other collective been advertised as a great advantage.

The state conference on families turned out to be a great clash between such half-truths. The scene had been set for what the Germans call a *Kulturkampf*—a battle between rival cultures. Those in charge found that they hadn't organized a conference so much as a provocation. Despite all outward differences, the people pouring out of the buses reminded one of another group that feels its traditional culture and spiritual values threatened by evil forces. In the Middle East, the devil is called Westernization; here it is Secular Humanism. But the impetus for both revolts is much the same. And those trying to ignore it here may prove as effective as the Shah of Iran, and infected with some of the same hubris.

Perhaps this whole imbroglio should have been expected. By the time a society gets around to holding a conference on one of its norms, it may no longer be a norm. The fight at the conference over defining the family may have been of more than abstract interest. Once the definition of the family embraces communes, boarding houses, homosexual liaisons, singles, or whatever, then the focus of such a conference is blurred. Those who make such arrangements, like everyone else, may have problems that need attention, but if so, let them find their own conference.

These conferences boil down to a bunch of querulous people sitting around being talked to by the Experts. (Whether anyone can really be an expert on an institution as generalized as the family is another question; it's a bit like being an expert on life.) It would be a bigger help to the family if, by the time the national conference arrived, it gathered together all these experts, bureaucrats, politicians, and Ph.D's of all persuasions and had them listen to a few families. At this conference, very little of the essence of family life seemed to come through the statistical reports and political proposals.

And so, like the Texan who found himself at a funeral where nary a soul had anything good to say about the late guest of honor, and therefore proposed to say a few words about Texas, I take the liberty of saying a few words for the family. They will not be original, for what they say was once so widely understood that there was no need to spell the message out. But what was once understood may now have to be explained—which is another symptom of the family's decay. But to proceed:

Young humans require the longest period of nurturing and dependence of any species, and the family has the longest, most reliable, most economical, and most effective record at doing just that. The family, as someone once observed, is a department of health, education, and welfare that works—if it can be kept working. The family is a microcosm of society that may continually mold its individual members to each other, leading them to discover that most efficient and sustaining and enduring connection between human beings: Love. The fleeting satisfactions of Looking Out for Number One may perhaps be sold in the larger society. But its allure tends to be undermined and exposed with some regularity in the family circle.

The family may be one of the few honest mirrors left in a society distorted by facile fashions in ideas, ways, behaviors. It can be the greatest school for the individual—when it works. The family can force people into a self-knowledge that can be gained in perhaps no other enterprise. It is a redoubt of privacy and re-creation, and a social model as well. In the context of family, people are capable of a heroism, accomplishment and devotion scarcely imaginable in other spheres. That is, you couldn't pay anyone to do the things fathers and mothers will do for free, and with joy.

How can these old possibilities be brought home once again? One begins to despair of doing it through conferences, or other forms of government-financed intervention. The churning wheels of the great Leviathan that is the welfare state may be of great utility in helping the individual, and, when the individual benefits, that may be reflected in family life. But one should be wary of submitting the essence of family life to a mass of wheels and gears. Government can render first aid in the case of family breakdown, it can give the family a good leaving alone, it can encourage the objective study and appreciation of the family, but *it cannot replace the family* and it should not try.

In the end, any political solution to the problems of the American family may prove tangential. Its current problems may stem from the surrounding, and at times enveloping, culture. Professor James Hitchcock at St. Louis University describes the challenge of contemporary culture to the family this way:

"While practically all sociologists have recognized that historically the family has been the backbone of human society, and that most people are part of the larger society primarily through their membership in a family, contemporary culture seems determined to treat the family as an accidental, even unimportant, institution, a community to which people may or may not choose to belong and which will also permit them to choose the degree of their participation.

"The model of humanity which is being proposed is a quite familiar one, although its full implications are rarely spelled out. It is the atomistic notion of society in which people are essentially on their own, linked to others only by tenuous threads. Thus human relationships hitherto thought sacred and unbreakable are increasingly broken almost routinely, and people are encouraged to find their identities not in the intimacy of close commitments but in the impersonal and atomized world of achievement. There is a particular and not very comforting view of human nature implied here, despite all the superficially cheerful rhetoric about happiness and fulfillment. It is a view of man as isolated, self-absorbed, and never finally trusting of anyone."

This is perhaps to overdraw the danger to the family, or the trend of the larger culture. But the danger signs the professor cites are readily apparent in the muddied stream of American consciousness— in education, conversation, advertising, mod theology, and in the whole range of—phony word for a phony concept—Lifestyles. In this cultural context, conferences on families that focus only on certain political and social programs may prove inconsequential. And those who direct their ire at the politicians and bureaucrats in charge of such conferences may be engaging in an act of righteous irrelevance.

The challenge to the family is broader. Its defenders and promoters are faced by a cultural attitude that permeates much of American society. This means all of us need to put in a few good words, and deeds, for the American family whenever we can—and say aloud what so many of us surely still understand.

Is There a Just Peace?

It was an uncomfortable setting because it was so comfortable. Here we were at ease in Zion, or rather in Pine Bluff's impressive First Presbyterian Church, which was a lot safer than Zion during the war against Iraq. Surrounded by friends and good feelings, we settled in for a proper panel discussion on the subject: "Is There a Just War?"

How strange to be talking of war in this church, where my daughter had taken violin lessons since she was old enough to hold the violin. Here we had listened to chamber music in the great room with the full Georgian windows. You could still almost hear the strains of Mozart, timeless, yet part of a time when war was an intermittence and a profession, not a posionous cloud that might descend any time. Talk about war here?

I kept thinking of my mother. Her life and therefore mine had been shaped in the mud and chaos of Poland during the First World War. She had tried to tell me about it, again, during one of our last conversations, when she could barely hold her head up. She didn't have the words but War, she wanted me to know, was the same everywhere: terrible, stupid, wasteful, suddenly and utterly devastating. It knows no boundaries of time or place, language or race. It is a great leveler, like Death. And what it teaches, you don't forget. Some things you want to tell your children before you die so they don't forget. I wondered what she would think of our polite discussion about organized slaughter. Imagine her reaction to a group of well-dressed folks sitting down to discuss war in a spacious meeting room after a nice church supper. Ah, America!

Much as she taught us to hate war, there are things worse. I still remember the scream from the back bedroom one peaceful Southern evening when I was a child. It seemed to go on so long. That was wartime, too, and there had been some whispered speculation among the grown-ups about what was happening to the Jews of Europe. Some fool had let the word slip in my grandmother's presence. Bubba Rosa had left all the rest of her family there—my mother's sisters and their families. The scream seemed to go on forever.

I also remember my reaction. I waited and waited for it to stop, then decided to ignore it. It was just one more strange thing adults did that children weren't supposed to notice. Almost 50 years later, I still hear it. The suddenness of it, the unendingness of it.

Now I hear myself on a church panel pontificating about war, methodically going through Augustine's list of requirements for a just war, as if this were a classroom exercise:

—Is there a just cause for this war? Yes. It has existed since the day Iraq invaded Kuwait. Its people would scream for more than five months before the world responded.

—Have we been guided by right intention? Yes. None of the allies in this widespread coalition covets Iraq as a colony; the intention is to liberate Kuwait, not enslave another nation.

—Has this war been approved by competent authority? Yes, after months of national debate and a formal vote in Congress.

—Will the good to be achieved outweigh the evil inherent in using force? Every day Saddam Hussein still controlled Kuwait, every day he attacked not only Saudi Arabia and Israel but the very birds of the air and fishes of the sea, the evil was committed anew. The way in which he conducted this war demonstrated why it had to be fought.

—Is there a reasonable chance of success? It would certainly seem so from the battlefield reports.

—Has force been used only as a last resort? Yes, after a dozen United Nations resolutions and an embargo that wasn't making much of a difference.

A better question for our panel might have been: Could there be a just peace if Saddam Hussein were *not* fought? It is not only war that must be just, but peace—or war will come soon enough.

Would there be peace if we had chosen not to fight Saddam Hussein? If we had decided to let the screams of his victims die out in silence?

A Toast to the Family

Leo Tolstoy said it: "Happy families are all alike; every unhappy family is unhappy in its own way." Leo Tolstoy said a lot of things. As the good ol' boy said on reading that day's "Li'l Orphan Annie," I don't believe but about half of that.

I was reading a dull yet provocative book—*America in Perspective: Major Trends in the United States Through the 1990s*—on the way to the happiest of family gatherings: a golden wedding anniversary. The book is so provocative because it is so dull; it's largely beside any moral point, and committed to statistics and their projection instead of vision and its realization. Naturally I would rather think of Tolstoy, who could make dullness interesting, or at least realistic.

The book is assigned reading for a seminar I'm supposed to attend in a couple of weeks; I don't want you to think I would have chosen it myself. If it were just an honest statistical abstract, it wouldn't be so bad, but it is full of hedged predictions and unhedged arrogance. It will probably make amusing reading in the year 2000—but not until then. The literature of futurism is at its best when it can be read as history that didn't happen. In the summer of 1987, I'd rather think about Tolstoy and family reunions.

The bride being celebrated at this anniversary dinner in New Orleans is my cousin Ann. I tend to forget whether we are actually related or just kissin' cousins. At every family reunion she patiently explains our convoluted but actual cousinhood, and I feel better for it. Not that it would matter with Ann; everybody is family around her—happy family. In addition to her four children and their families, the room is full of cousins actual and honorary, friends, and neighbors— including some who lived next door to her in Shreveport who knows how many years ago. There is something about Ann and her bride- groom, Pinky, that you'd go a ways to be around, and that you'd like your children to see and feel. We brought the kids along, and my sister and her husband have come down from New York.

Ann was my father's most successful import. He had come to Shreveport to go into the second-hand shoe business, and boarded with Pinky's family his first weeks in town. To an orthodox Jew like my father, there was something scandalous about a young man's still being single at 29—especially if there was a beautiful and marriageable cousin waiting in Chicago. So Ann was invited down, there was a watermelon party, and nature took its course with only a slight nudge from Ben Greenberg. Now I was sampling a good vintage and looking down at the lights of New Orleans, surrounded by the children, grandchildren and the general bounty of that match my father made half a century ago. A shoemaker, he could always find a mate for a single.

Cousin Pinky was born a salesman. He was selling the sizzle and not the steak years before I heard that phrase in journalism school. For years, he and Ann had lived in a little town on the Louisiana side of the Mississippi River, where he was in the liquor business. But there's something meaner than a fellow who'll vote a town dry and then leave it, and that's a whole state that'll vote itself wet without the least consideration for those who sell spirits just the other side of the state line. Pinky and Ann had wound up in New Orleans, where he sells Italian wines now, surrounded by his children and children's children.

The wine this evening was fine, but not nearly as intoxicating as the nostalgia—or the language. I noticed that Pinky's North-Louisiana Southron has acquired a slight admixture of Cajun over the years, just as his extended family now has. For lagniappe, there was my sister's remarkable accent. She had spoken only Yiddish before entering public school, and had married a New Yorker stationed at the nearby air base during the war. The result was a basic Southern drawl with a Yiddish locution ("To the party y'all'll come!") and an overlay of Yankee of the Lung-Island variety. This doesn't count the bits of Arabic she picked up on Shreveport's Texas Avenue, where we grew up with a lot of Lebanese kids whose families also lived above their stores.

Contrary to Count Tolstoy, no two families happy or unhappy may be just alike, but there's nothing like a 50th wedding anniversary to remind one of how similar all families are. The memories of the old and hopes of the young mingle, and an enlarged photograph of the bridal couple fifty years ago inspires the same gasp of delight and admiration. I notice that, regardless of age, social status or income, my family remains uniformly middle class. Some of the young people may betray signs of incipient intellectualism, but that handicap tends to fade with age and leave us almost normal.

Like my sister's language, the gathering was pure American, that is, a wild mixture. In the plane on the way back, I come across one of the few humorous passages in my required reading, even if the humor is of the unconscious variety. The distinguished scholars who produced this study seem to have concluded that the latest wave of immigrants to this country can't be absorbed—a conclusion reached by every generation of Americans back to the Indians.

According to this latest version, "Hispanic-Americans seem much less disposed than previous migrants to commit themselves to full acceptance of the American way of life. This is true of all Third World immigrants to the USA; Hispanics are most important because they are by far the largest group. Spanish language, culture and history, Latin-American Catholicism, male dominance and low levels of inter-marriage combine to keep Hispanic migrants apart."

Uh huh. With appropriate changes, this is the kind of prose one finds in genteel nativist pamphlets at the turn of the century, when immigrants from Eastern and Southern Europe were flocking into the country—other peoples of strange tongue. The distinguished creators of this latest study are described as "a specialized research and consulting firm drawing on over three hundred senior faculty members at Oxford University and other leading universities around the world...." I wish they would set aside their purely statistical projections for just one emotionally sane evening, and attend a golden wedding anniversary in New-Orleans-the-Land-of-Dreams. They might learn something about America, and about the American dream.

11 | On Religion

Our Spiritual Amnesia

Arthur Schlesinger Jr., the son of a great American historian, delivered a peevish address at Brown University in which he unburdened himself of various crosses that American gliberals must bear, principally the resurgence of religious values in American life. Nothing irritates a glib more than the sneaking suspicion that the ideals he holds dearest may have religious roots; it's so disconcerting a thesis that he may profess to be amused by it. Professor Schlesinger's scorn for that notion is more than sweeping; it's encyclopedic:

"As a historian, I confess to a certain amusement when I hear the Judeo-Christian tradition praised as the source of our concern for human rights. In fact, the great religious ages were notable for their indifference to human rights in the contemporary sense. They were notorious not only for acquiescence in poverty, inequality, exploitation and oppression but for enthusiastic justifications of slavery, persecution, abandonment of small children, torture, genocide..." and so shrilly on.

To read this catalogue of religion's sins is to be impressed mainly by the animus of the cataloguer. That last sin, genocide, was not even a word before this century, which surely no one would confuse with a great religious age; the term had to be introduced to describe the modern, systematic murder of a whole people. Can Professor Schlesinger

27

be under the impression that the Third Reich was some sort of theocracy?

No matter. On he hurtles: "Human rights is not a religious idea. It is a secular idea, the product of the last four centuries of Western history." So much for the Exodus God who leads His people from slavery into freedom. So much for proclaiming liberty throughout the land. So much for the Hebrew Prophets. ("What mean ye that ye beat my people to pieces and grind the faces of the poor?...Is not this what I require of you as a fast: to loose the fetters of injustice, to untie the knots of the yoke, to snap every yoke and set free those who have been crushed?") And so much for the Teacher from Nazareth, who enjoined: "Inasmuch as ye have done it unto one of the least of these my brethren, ye have done it unto me."

Professor Schlesinger may be concerned only with human rights "in the contemporary sense," as he vaguely says. But those rights are traceable to a belief in "the laws of Nature and Nature's God," to quote a document of some importance in American history. Some have called the Declaration of Independence the quintessential expression of the American idea, and at its heart is this remarkable and not very secular attribution of human rights:

"We hold these truths to be self-evident, that all men are created equal, that they are endowed by their Creator with certain unalienable Rights, that among these are Life, Liberty and the pursuit of Happiness. That to secure these rights, Governments are instituted among Men, deriving their just powers from the consent of the governed. That whenever any Form of Government becomes destructive of these ends, it is the Right of the People to alter or to abolish it, and to institute new Government."

Wow. Talk about your religious fanatics. That kind of talk is revolutionary. The Founding Fathers seem to have had pronounced ideas about the Author of liberty, and by that they surely didn't mean George III, Parliament, or the last few centuries of Western history. But the Declaration of Independence, the hard-pressed professor points out, was "written by political, not by religious leaders"—as if political leaders could not be moved by religious ideas. As if religion were limited to the clergy. Equally tricky is his definition of Naziism and Communism as "totalitarian social religions" rather than the profoundly anti-religious movements they were. Compared to the professor's intellectual intolerance, Jerry Falwell would sound broad-minded.

In Arthur Schlesinger's narrow little cosmology, there would seem room only for secular prophets. How do you suppose he manages to ignore the distinctly religious inclinations of a Dietrich Bonhoeffer or Martin Luther King Jr.? Does he think the connection between the civil rights movement of this century and the black church was wholly a coincidence? Has he noticed that abolitionism was not exactly a secular movement? Can he have mistaken the "Battle Hymn of the Republic" for a secular anthem? Does he consider all such instances of religious influence only incidental? That may be the very definition of a gliberal: someone who mistakes the essential for the incidental. And vice versa.

One of the reasons gliberals twist themselves into such unseemly postures is that they don't seem able to recognize the idea of the holy outside the church, as if the sense of the sacred could not exist beyond stained glass.

When he speaks of the current controversy over the desecration of the flag, Professor Schlesinger puts inverted commas around the word "desecration"—as if to deny that a secular symbol could inspire reverence. It's a common enough theme in the debate over flag-burning. And what a pitifully limited concept of the sacred it reveals. It is not enough for the gliberal that church and state be separate (a saving principle of both government and of religious life) but society and religion must also be.

Yet what goes on in the courtroom, the family, the schoolhouse—yes, even in politics—can also partake of the holy. Mr. Lincoln was not bound by so circumscribed a view of the sacred when he said of the battle-field at Gettysburg: "The brave men, living and dead, who struggled here, have consecrated it far above our poor power to add or detract."

But the professor, with his tin ear in matters of the spirit, doubtless would find such ideas amusing. As he confidently pro-claims, "Human rights is not a religious idea." He quotes that wonderful passage from *Huckleberry Finn* in which Huck decides that he would rather go to Hell than turn in his friend Jim, the fugitive slave. Professor Schlesinger doesn't see in that decision an act of grace, of love, of irrepressible, unarguable, irrational religion.

Granted, Huck's decision ain't theology, or at least not the respectable theology he's acquired, but it sure as Hell is religion. It comes just after he has grasped an essential truth about prayer: "I was trying to make my mouth *say* I would do the right thing and the clean thing, and go and write to that nigger's owner and tell where he was; but deep down in me I knowed it was a lie, and He knowed it. You can't pray a lie—I found that out."

All this is lost on our professor, who is willing enough to concede the social usefulness of religion (he quotes Chesterton) but announces that human rights was invented 400 years ago. That sure and solemn assertion, rolled out professorially at a ceremonious convocation of an Ivy League university, would make the loudest, Bible-thumpingest tent preacher in Arkansas seem worldly-wise.

The Death of an Idea

For years now the concept of perjury has been ailing in the Western world. Those who follow the fortunes of arcane ideas should be informed that not long ago it died in the land where it took shape. An official inquiry in Israel reported that, for the past 16 years, officials of that country's security service have been routinely perjuring themselves in order to convict suspected terrorists.

The reaction was much as one would expect from a modern, advanced society. The commission recommended that no one be punished, or dismissed, or censured in any way. The conclusion of this official investigation could be summed up as: Don't do it any more. And so due respect was paid to the late concept that lying under oath is wrong; it is possible that convictions obtained through perjured testimony might even be reviewed. But the revelation set off no great public clamor. It was as if most Israelis knew what their security service had been doing all along, and had no objection. There's a war on, isn't there?

The Israeli army officer whose conviction set off the inquiry is a Moslem by the name of Ifat Nafus. He is Israel's own Alfred Dreyfus, whose conviction on the basis of false evidence divided France for much of the last century. The Dreyfus Affair became one of the great watersheds and wounds of modern European history. But there will be no Nafus Affair in this more advanced century; perjury isn't that big a deal any more.

The Israeli inquiry concluded that the officials who perjured themselves never had "meant to convict innocent persons." It just worked out that way. Those who swore the defendant in this case had voluntarily confessed doubtless had come to think of perjury as a routine necessity, another technical requirement of modern life.

On the travel posters, Israel is still the Land of the Bible. That's the book in which it is written: *Who shall ascend the mountain of the Lord? And who shall stand in his holy place? He that has clean hands and a pure heart, who has not taken God's name in vain, and has not sworn deceitfully.* But the modern man who studies the Bible as literature knows a poetic fancy when he hears one. He is not about to jeopardize the security of the state because of a technicality, especially an ancient—and therefore outmoded—one.

It is not only in Israel that a technicality has come to mean any right that stands in the way of a conviction. Wasn't it an attorney general of the United States, The Honorable Edwin Meese, who said that only the guilty avail themselves of their rights in a criminal investigation? (If so, surely he said that before he became enmeshed in one.)

While truthfulness may be paid homage in public statements, as it was by this Israeli commission, perjury is a tough rap to prove, as was observed in the midst of Watergate. That was the affair in which the conspirator-in-chief, Richard Nixon, told the public one thing ("I condemn any attempts to cover up this case, no matter who is involved") and his colleagues another. ("I want you all to stonewall it, let them plead the Fifth Amendment, cover up, or anything else.") *Anything else.* The truth has an inconvenient way of complicating not only criminal convictions but political ambitions.

What's wrong with a little perjury in a good cause, anyway? The concept that perjury is an ultimate wrong becomes foreign to modern, pragmatic societies. Such a stricture has become inconvenient, and therefore disposable in the throwaway society. The Iran-Contra affair was distinguished by various witnesses who were caught telling less than the truth, the whole truth, and nothing but the truth to Congress—a tendency that much of the public seemed to accept as proof of their patriotism.

When Robert Bolt wrote *A Man for All Seasons* about Sir Thomas More, he felt obliged to answer an obvious question in this age— "Why do I take as my hero a man who brings about his own death because he can't put his hand on an old black book and tell an ordinary lie?" The playwright tried to explain:

"A man takes an oath only when he wants to commit himself quite exceptionally to the statement, when he wants to make an identity between the truth of it and his own virtue; he offers himself as a guarantee. And it works. There is a special kind of shrug for a perjurer; we feel that the man has no self to offer. Of course it's much less effective now that for most of us the actual words of the oath are not much more than impressive mumbo-jumbo than it was when they made obvious sense; we would prefer most men to guarantee their statements with, say, cash rather than with themselves. We feel—we know—the self to be an equivocal commodity. There are fewer and fewer things which, as they say, we 'cannot bring ourselves' to do. We can find almost no limits for ourselves other than the physical, which, being physical, are not optional. Perhaps this is why we have fallen back so widely on physical torture as a means of bringing pressure to bear on another..."

This may explain why the report by the Israeli commission, headed by a former Supreme Court justice of that country, also countenances physical force to extract confessions. Accept perjury as routine and soon enough other limits fade.

What must the Israeli officer who was imprisoned for seven years on perjured testimony have thought of the commission's conclusions? Said Ifat Nafus: "I had anticipated that the people responsible for putting me in prison and ruining my life would be brought to trial. Instead I see that they are going to go free." He had only one question: "What about justice?"

Well, that's one of those other concepts that may have to go when perjury becomes routine—a necessary bother rather than an ultimate betrayal. As Robert Bolt noted, once the idea of a transcendent self is lost, the perjurer betrays nothing. Unless perjury is a sin against something sacred in man, how serious a crime can it be? What, if anything, is betrayed if the self has become an equivocal commodity? Despite all his learning and sophistication and love of life, Thomas More preferred to lose his head rather than his self. His was a medieval choice and, however much moderns may admire it, we may no longer be able to understand it. Instead, in an arrogance of arrogances, we tend to use the term medieval as a synonym for backward.

Church into State

Now and then a passing comment in the news will define the spirit of the age, or rather the absence of spirit.

But who would have picked Bill McCuen as the source of such illumination? He's the secretary of state of Arkansas, and that job is seldom a source of controversy, let alone illumination. His general political philosophy has been to follow the path of least resistance, and that has been enough to keep him out of trouble until called upon to exercise independent judgment. Yet from just such an innocent may come the one comment that defines an age.

What is it that he said of such import? It was a brief comment tacked on to the annual story about what the secretary of state planned to do, if anything, about the Nativity scene at the state Capitol. Across the country, such interviews with uneasy public officials who are caught between following their constituents or the law have become the first harbingers of the season to be jolly, beating out even department store Santas and pre-pre-Christmas sales.

Here's the statement from Secretary McCuen that may sum up the *Zeitgeist*—and also the next direction of Supreme Court decisions on church-state issues. It appeared in the last paragraph of an interview, added as if only an afterthought: "The Arkansas display incorporates the theme of Christmas and not just the Nativity of Christ."

Here's a way to leave Christ in Christmas but add so much more. It puts the religious thing in perspective. What's being celebrated is not just the theme of the Nativity (God made man, and come to redeem the sins of the world) but the theme of Christmas. The same theme the Japanese celebrate so elaborately: the holiday itself. They may not share or even know the religious significance of the day but they clearly think it's a neat occasion and have smoothly incorporated it into their social calendar and marketing plans—like so many Americans.

In his own unconscious way, Bill McCuen may have summed up the new, constitutionally approved way to celebrate Christmas: not as some particularistic religious celebration limited to believers, but as a cultural artifact that belongs to all. It's not "just" the Nativity but the theme of Christmas that counts! And what is that theme? No need to go into detail and dredge up awkward constitutional questions about an establishment of religion. Let's be content to mention Peace on Earth and Good Will toward Men—without emphasizing who first delivered that message, or on what occasion. Instead, let's have a grand birthday party without overemphasizing Whose birthday it is. Why complicate matters?

The desacralization of religious symbols proceeds almost as rapidly as the sacralization of secular rituals. The presumptuous words "under God" were slipped into the Pledge of Allegiance only recently and now the Pledge can be recited at a national political convention with the devotion of the Apostles' Creed. Just who or what is being worshipped may remain vague, but that's what happens when a political party grows dissatisfied with the usual political rites and reaches out for religious symbolism. Only later may some wonder why the old religious symbols don't seem to have the same power and meaning any more now that the state has expropriated them.

The Supreme Court of the United States already has agreed to take another look at the question of whether a local government can put up a nativity scene or a menorah. One can almost foresee Whizzer White's majority opinion now, in which he explains that Christmas and Hanukkah are not just religious holidays but cultural institutions in American society, and so may be duly celebrated by government. ("The display incorporates the theme of Christmas/Hanukkah and not just the Nativity-of-Christ/miracle-of-the-lights.") Arkansas' secretary of state may not have ignored the law of the land but only anticipated it.

It seems to be the nature of expanding government: A secular state cannot remain content within its own limited sphere; it must reach out for the power and the glory. But although the state may covet the symbols of religion, it certainly doesn't want to identify itself with any explicit confession of faith. That would be religion—and all the state seeks is religiosity. In their own way, those who argue that the display of these symbols on public property has nothing to do with religion make a valid point.

Well, what's wrong with using sacred symbols in a secular setting? A naked public square does seem to bother some folks; it cries out for decoration the way a restaurant needs ambiance. Fair is fair: Look at all the mod theologians who use secular success as a religious proof. Is it any wonder that secular society would like to acquire a few religious talismans, suitably nonsectarian, maybe one for each of The Major Religions? You don't have to be Catholic to wear a St. Christopher medal—or to admire Nativity scenes.

Good ol' Bill McCuen said it, doubtless in all innocence: These displays incorporate a theme, not "just" religion.

He has summed up the highly adulterated spirit of the age.

Unholy Spectacle

For a time it looked as though Bill McCuen, the Arkansas secretary of state, had taken an unshakable lead in the national competition to keep Christ out of Christmas. Defending the constitutionality of the nativity scene he installed at the state Capitol, Mr. McCuen explained: "We're not celebrating the birth of Christ, we're just celebrating Christmas." For sheer insensitivity in the Category of Church-and-State, Mixtures Thereof, he seemed to have all comers beat.

But now Mr. McCuen has got some distinguished competition: President John E. Brown III of John Brown University in Siloam Springs, Arkansas. Dr. Brown's approach is more subtle (it couldn't be any more direct than Bill McCuen's) but a recent essay of his delivers the same message. The university president concludes his case for making the Holy Family public property with these words: "It is a sad commentary that, in a nation beset by crime, crack and crying children, some federal courts should find mere symbols of religious faith to be offensive to the public good."

Almost visible between the lines is the message that religion would make a useful antidote to social problems, specifically Crime, Crack, and Crying Children. This is the well known case for God on the grounds of social utility—although those making it seldom state it so candidly. They may prefer to say that classroom prayer, for example, should be reinstituted in the public schools because it would raise grades, help with discipline, and cut down on sexual promiscuity.

Among the motives seldom if ever listed is the greater glory of God. That would be too explicit. God has become something of an embarrassment in polite society, let alone in constitutional law. When the holy must be justified solely by secular standards, as in a courtroom, any mention of Him tends to be prudently eliminated from arguments in His defense. Note that the introduction of "Creation Science" in the public schools was formally defended on grounds of Science rather than as obedience to the Creator.

The phrase of President Brown's that sticks in the mind, and throat, is his reference to the "mere symbols of religious faith." It brings to mind a letter that young Flannery O'Connor wrote a friend in 1955 about a conversation that had occurred when she was even younger:

"I was once, five or six years ago, taken by some friends to have dinner with Mary McCarthy and her husband, Mr. Broadwater.... She departed the Church at age 15 and is a Big Intellectual. We went at eight and at one, I hadn't opened my mouth once, there being nothing for me in such company to say. The people who took me were Robert Lowell and his now wife, Elizabeth Hardwick. Having me there was like having a dog present who had been trained to say a few words but overcome with inadequacy had forgotten them. Well, toward morning the conversation turned on the Eucharist, which I, being the Catholic, was obviously supposed to defend. Mrs. Broadwater said when she was a child and received the Host, she thought of it as the Holy Ghost, He being the 'most portable' person of the Trinity; now she thought of it as a symbol and implied that it was a pretty good one. I then said, in a very shaky voice, 'Well, if it's a symbol, to hell with it.' That was all the defense I was capable of but I realize now that this is all I will ever be able to say about it, outside of a story, except that it is the center of existence for me; all the rest of life is expendable."

As a storyteller, Miss O'Connor was just finding her voice and her stride but clearly she had found her faith some time before, the essence of which is to observe the line between the sacred and the profane, between the expendable and essential, the symbolic and the real.

It is a line that keeps fading in a society that elevates religiosity but is not about to take up religion. That is, if it can still distinguish between the two.

The state's incorporation of the church's rites is by now a process so familiar it may no longer be noticed. First the holy becomes a symbol and then a "mere symbol," until what is symbolized becomes difficult to see beyond a vague, innocuous agreeability. One name for this process is trivialization. Another is profanation.

The denigration of the sacred has seldom been described more smoothly than by President Brown: "Nativity scenes on public grounds had been thought to be a traditional part of the Christmas season. The inclusion of European holiday customs added to the general theme of community celebration, giving people of all faiths, or nonfaith, an equal opportunity to proclaim joy and peace to men of good will." This is a much more scholarly and elevated explanation than Bill McCuen's pathetically transparent "We're not celebrating the birth of Christ, we're just celebrating Christmas." On the whole, I prefer Mr. McCuen's version. It's shorter and clearer. And it faces the issue directly.

The issue, though it may no longer be recognized because the religious sensibilities of society have been so dulled, is how far the state should go in profaning the holy. It now has become the regular business of courts to decide when religion has entered the public domain. That point is reached when the church's rites and symbols become so general, so inoffensive, so undemanding, that they do not risk establishing religion, and so may be appropriated by the state. It's a little like the way aspirin became a common noun instead of a trademark.

A line of half-comic, half-appalling court decisions now begins to delineate where the sacred and profane meet, or maybe mesh. It's the sort of exercise in grotesquerie that would appeal to Flannery O'Connor, who had an eye for the generally accepted abomination. The courts now have ruled that if a Hanukkah menorah on public property is part of only a cultural display, it is constitutionally kosher. If the Holy Family is exhibited as part of a general Christmas display along with Santa and his elves, that is constitutional, too (Lynch v. Donnelly, 1984). Only adulterated forms of religion are allowed.

It speaks well of President Brown that he flinches at the thought of a nativity scene having to be erected "between a flashing reindeer nose and a talking wishing well" in order to be constitutional. But that is the logical result of the process he has wound up defending— the process of desacralizing the sacred. So does faith become symbol and even the symbol "mere." Flannery O'Connor said it: If it's a symbol, to Hell with it.

The Bible: Does It Belong in School?

It happens all over the country. Some school district gives the Bible a lick and a promise in its curriculum—a daily verse is read over the public address system, for example—and the school system is promptly threatened with a lawsuit. Whereupon the administration explains that the practice is harmless. (How's that for a stirring defense of Bible study?) Then, after a few barks from some high-strung constitutional watchdog like the American Civil Liberties Union, the school district backs off. Bible readings are banned and the story ends with somebody in charge blaming the press for having blown the whistle in the first place. And all's confused that ends confused.

That's the way it happened at the high school in Blytheville, Ark., which stopped offering a Bible verse along with the daily announcements. This unhappy ending left the usual misimpressions, among them that the Supreme Court of the United States has banned the Bible from the public schools. It hasn't. From its first, misunderstood ruling on this question, the court not only has approved but encouraged teaching about religion in the schools; what it has banned is *preaching* religion in the schools. There is a difference, but to notice it requires that rarest of virtues in academe: common sense.

Turning a public school classroom into a prayer service is an establishment of religion, said the court, stating the obvious. Studying a book like the Bible (or the Koran, or the Bhagavad Gita) isn't. For that matter, studying religion itself isn't unconstitutional. The court's object was to promote the separation of church and state, not of student and knowledge.

The high school principal in Blytheville may have been on constitutionally sound ground when he defended reciting Bible verses to start the school day. "We don't try to interpret the Scriptures and give them specific meanings," Bruce Young explained. "If we did, then there would be a problem. But we just simply read it." He would probably have been on sounder ground if the Biblical verses alternated with quotations from other religions' Scriptures, or from Shakespeare and other literary works. Then there would have been less question about whether, by reading from the Bible, the state was establishing a religion.

But the case for Bible study won't be tested in this instance because the school district won't stand up for the principal's interpretation of the law, or alter its practice to make it clearer that the school was trying to educate, not indoctrinate, its students. It's easier to blame the press and give up.

Whatever lessons a verse-a-day might have taught the students, what will they learn from this behavior on the part of their elders? Will they learn that, when pressed, it's best to sacrifice one's beliefs and shift responsibility to that convenient scapegoat, the Media? (As in: "The media made us do it!")

Underlying these misimpressions may be a far more serious misassumption: that a daily Bible verse, administered like a daily vitamin pill, will keep evil away. If the Bible teaches anything, it is that the Old Gentleman who goes to and fro in the land is not so easily evaded. To treat Scripture as a kind of immunization against drugs, teenage pregnancy and bad study habits is unscriptural—besides being simple-minded. If that's the purpose of Bible reading, its advocates are bound to be disappointed; the Bible is a book, not a magic spell. And to use it to further our own social or political or personal agenda, rather than let it speak and risk its shaping us, is a kind of sacrilege of its own.

To quote Martin Marty, historian of religion and bemused observer of what is happening in its name: "To promote religion in the curriculum as the remedy for 'why Johnny can't pray,' would be false advertising and ultimately disappointing." Religion needs to be studied in the schools, not simply used. It's an exciting, interesting, essential—some would say quintessential—part of the human condition, not one more prophylactic.

Far from being too much, reciting a Bible verse a day is too little exposure to religion in the schools. Would any school district propose to teach mathematics by broadcasting an algebraic formula a day over the public address system? Or history by giving students one historic date every morning? Or language by reciting a quote a day from Bartlett's? Biblical illiteracy needs to be combatted the same way other kinds are: through study.

This is not to endorse Bible study as a branch of literature, though the two have much in common. To study the Bible as one would study Shakespeare is also to be ultimately disappointed. The Bible is no more literature than the Book of Job is a Greek tragedy. The Bible goes beyond literature or, to put it more accurately, it resists becoming literature. It has literary qualities yet it is something more (doubters might say something less), but in the end it is surely something different.

In Defense of the King James

The last place I talked to a great Bible scholar was in a stretch of piney woods a few miles outside Utica, Mississippi. He was Harry Orlinsky, a scholar and translator who had been in on more than one of the landmark revisions of the English Bible this century. Dr. Orlinsky could discuss Akkadian folklore, his part in unraveling the Dead Sea Scrolls, or the pool games of his youth with equal zest. He was, in short, a most impressive man. That weekend in the woods, he was down from Hebrew Union College to address a retreat at a Reform Jewish camp.

After hearing about Biblical parallels with the Ugaritic and the wonders of the *vav*-converse tense in Hebrew, and being respectfully mystified, I had one question for Dr. Orlinsky: In light of all the more modern, accurate translations of the Bible, how does the old King

James Version still retain its awesome power despite any number of revisions? Dr. Orlinsky looked at me sympathetically, the way one might at a romantic unaware even of the source of his romanticism, and explained, simply enough: "Because you're used to it."

I demurred, but not very well. All I had was a feeling about the words, and inarticulate emotion is no match for Dr. Orlinsky's science. Maybe it really was the attraction of familiarity, as he explained, but I didn't believe it for a minute. Surely if one placed the old passages from the Authorized Version side by side with some of the newer translations, even someone who had never heard them before would recognize the power and the glory—the Elizabethan bounty—of the King James Version. "Yea, though I walk through the valley of the shadow of death, I will fear no evil" has to be superior to a version in the Jewish Publication Society's translation, "though I walk through a valley of the deepest darkness." Or the Anchor Bible's equally modern, "Even though I should walk through the midst of total darkness."

Nor may the new versions necessarily be more literal, as the editor of the Anchor notes in a conscientious footnote. (Another great advantage of the King James is the absence of footnotes. Apparently it is only modern poetry, *a la* T. S. Eliot, that requires them.) In the New English Bible, Joseph's coat of many colors has been demoted, for no clear reason, to "a long, sleeved robe." Gentle Reader will no doubt have his own favorite example of this style of Biblical translation, which might be dubbed Modern Drab. Why, for example, change "How are the mighty fallen!" in the King James to "How have the mighty fallen!" or, worse, "How are the men of war fallen!"

These are only some of the clinkers cited by another student of the Hebrew Bible, Chaim Raphael, in his review of one of the new translations. One is also indebted to him for a succinct explanation of why modern translations may not come up to the King James. Much of the language of the Hebrew Bible, Chaim Raphael explains, "runs counter to every effort to express it in a modern idiom" because by the time its words were set down, they were already archaic and had the power and mystery of ancient words.

And he goes on to note: "In this regard, the Bible was well served, it would seem, by the King James Version, which was in an English archaic even when first published in 1611, since it was heavily influenced by Coverdale's Bible of 1535." So that it can be said of the King James Version, as Chaim Raphael says of the Hebrew Bible, that its words and rhythms were "undoubtedly archaic to their own audience and doubly so to us, as if the force within them drew its authority from a historic miracle which transcended the workaday canons of clarity and reason and had to be absorbed through a cloud of mystery."

Chaim Raphael cites even the mistakes of the King James Version as an advantage: "The translators had a reverence for the text before them, however obscure. When they could not understand it, they would produce an apparently literal translation that was a stab in the dark, sometimes quite meaningless, but still carrying with it the splendid orotund tone of the version as a whole. For all these reasons, the KJV conveyed much of the archaism and mystery that is tangible in the original Hebrew."

Lovers of the King James Version who find themselves discomfited, not to say appalled, by some of today's endless re-revisions are indebted to Chaim Raphael for supplying a logical reason why—not that love necessarily requires logic. His explanation might also help those linguistic archaeologists understand the strong but not always articulated preference for the King James Version over the years. I just wish I had had Chaim Raphael out in the woods of Mississippi that day with Dr. Orlinsky. Science, meet Poetry.

Letter from Below

(With Apologies to C.S. Lewis)

June 4, 1990

My dear Wormwood,

The best of news. On the first anniversary of another of our great victories, the one in Tiananmen Square, your affectionate uncle happened to be glancing through the public prints, which are second only to television in promoting our cause, when my eye fell on the latest decision of the U.S. Supreme Court concerning church and state, both of which have been our province from time to time. It seems the distinguished justices have been busying themselves blurring the distinction between the two—a work that would be most dear to my heart if I had one.

This time the justices aren't deciding just when a religious symbol has become sufficiently irreligious to be displayed on public property (may they never tire of such work!) but rather how to make religion an extracurricular activity, which of course is what it should have been all along. What better way to keep it from being essential?

It shouldn't be long before the happy impression spreads that religion requires the support of the state, or at least the occasional use of a classroom. It's a start. Experience has shown that the more official a creed, the less appealing. See the paltry interest in the established churches of Western Europe. Or note the disaster that has befallen that most established of pseudo-religions, Communism, in the eastern part of the continent. It's enough to make you weep.

I loved Sandra Day O'Connor's formulation for the majority of the court: "A school that permits a student-initiated and student-led religious club to meet after school, just as it permits any other student group to do, does not convey a message of state approval or endorsement of the particular religion." Do you think she has any inkling of what it *does* convey—namely, state approval of religion in general? And a state that can approve religion can disapprove it, too. Indeed, I think approval is much the more effective way to stifle the thing.

Religion-in-general, my dear Wormwood, is our great ally. It should be encouraged at every turn. I can just see the kiddies sitting around homeroom now, deciding which after-school clubs to join. ("I just can't make a choice, can you, Rebecca Jo? Chess, scuba diving or religion, they all sound like fun. Maybe I'll take religion. They say it improves your communications skills.") It shouldn't be long before faith is treated as a nice, constructive after-school activity.

Religion, the real thing, can't be practiced in general—any more than language can be spoken in general. You have to choose a specific one. Religion-in-general has all the moral authority and emotional impact of Esperanto. Our mission is to replace belief with some safe, state-approved substitute. Once we extend a veneer of religiosity over the schools, the genuine article can be expected to fade away. Better to have the little suckers pray in school than in church or, even more dangerous, at home. Civil religion, that's the ticket, my dear nephew.

John Paul Stevens may represent something of a problem. Thank hell, he was the only dissenter from this lovely little ruling. Only he recognized that it comes "perilously close to an outright command to allow organized prayer...on school premises." Do you think he's on to our game, namely more and more organization, less and less personal prayer? We have to reduce prayer to something else—an extra-curricular activity, another government benefit, an opening ceremony, a public convenience...anything but an intimate experience. That's when it's dangerous.

Only when prayer and Bible study are officially recognized as wholesome activities conducive to better grades and order in the halls will we have defanged the saving thing. The trick is to make it an *instrument*—a technique, an extra-curricular activity, *never* a state of being, or all our subjects will be left open to the Enemy. We'll know we're succeeding when school Prayer Clubs start having their own letter jackets. What a great day it'll be when we make religion utterly dependent on peer pressure.

Justice O'Connor says a school can still ban disruptive groups. That's precisely the kind of prayer we want to encourage, Wormwood, the kind that doesn't disrupt anything, especially not our stock in trade: ordinary, routinely accepted, unnoticeable evil. Real prayer can be a powerfully disruptive influence. It can revolutionize the most stable society; never forget what befell poor Nineveh when its people unaccountably listened to that Jonah person against all reason. Yet prayer can also be the one thing that holds people together when everything else has collapsed around them. Perverse, unpredictable thing, prayer. It needs to be put in the care of the proper authorities, namely the state.

Isn't the name of the law that the court upheld perfect? The Equal Access Act of 1984. I love it. The great problem with the First Amendment, which so long has stood in our way, is precisely that it does *not* provide equal access to religion. Government is explicitly barred from passing any law having to do with its establishment. Religion is set apart, as if it were something holy. Government is told not to touch it or even come close to it. This is intolerable, Wormwood. Only by bringing religion under the state's authority, by rendering unto Caesar what isn't his, can we blur the essence of religion, which is the separation of the holy and the profane. This decision should help.

The great challenge facing religion is not equal access to the world but how to retain enough integrity to stay distinguishable from the world. My fellow demon Glittercut did a good night's work when he invented Success Theology. Our job, my young protégé, is to make religion *in*distinguishable from the world, one more extra-curricular activity. The last temptation—mastery of the powers and principalities—is still the most effective. As the world giveth, so give we.

What we've got to do is get people thinking of religion as something educational, beneficial, a means to some greater social end, an institution wholly worthy of a little government support—a tuition grant here and there, or a place to meet in the schools. We've got to get it on the dole. That way it won't go off on its own with unpredictable results. It needs to be woven smoothly into the social fabric so it can be corrupted with everything else. Left alone, there's no telling where it may spread. The Enemy can be dangerous when left to His own strange devices. Be warned, young demon, He is never stronger than when He appears weak in the eyes of the world.

Have you noticed the enthusiasm this ruling has kindled among many of the faithful? It's an inspiring sight. They've been handed a stone and think it's bread. Delicious.

That's about all the news from down under. I'm still vying with my old rival Gallclaws for the next GS-16 rating in the bureaucracy. The competition here is, of course, hellish. But news like this cheers me.

Your affectionate uncle,
Screwtape

A Word for the Gods

Addressing a group of students not long ago, Ronald Reagan delivered the now customary defense of prayer in the schools. The President told the kids he favored school prayer because "'I don't know anyone who was hurt by it.'" There have been stronger endorsements of milk toast.

But then the President really got rolling—all the way back to the Greeks and Romans. His warning echoed that of any commencement speaker inclined to use the decline and fall of Rome for his own purposes. The Greek and Roman civilizations began to collapse, said the President, "'when they deserted their gods.'" Which is pretty much what some ancients warned would happen when their contemporaries began taking up with exotic cults like Christianity. That judgment would be repeated centuries later in Edward Gibbon's *The Decline and Fall of the Roman Empire*, which traces the fall of Rome in large part to the subversive influence of that New Age religion from the East.

Now Ronald Reagan comes to the defense of the old gods, if perhaps unconsciously. The President's style may be less subtle than

Edward Gibbon's. The great English historian was subdued not only by a natural restraint but by those laws of the realm mandating criminal penalties for any open attack on Christianity, by then a state religion. Such laws are to be expected in societies that do not believe in the separation of church and state—an American principle that would be blurred if, as this president suggests, prayers were imposed on the public schools.

Ronald Reagan, whose equal in scholarship has not been seen in the White House since Warren G. Harding, may be unaware of the full implications of his comments, not to mention their distinguished lineage. That makes his views all the more charming. Unfortunately, what is only naive in a single individual can be goshawful in a chief executive charged with protecting the First Amendment, which takes a dim view of laws respecting an establishment of religion.

The religion that Mr. Reagan would establish (while claiming not to establish one, of course) would be a most general one—not a religion at all by the standards of strict ritual and doctrine, undeviating faith, or transcendent importance. This generalized religion is more like good manners or political ceremony, and is generally taken as such by American opinion. No wonder an American president can say a good word for the pagan gods, as Mr. Reagan did, and no one much notices. That's because he wasn't defending paganism but whatever religion exists in a society. Stick by your gods—that seemed to be his message—or else disaster will follow. When in Rome, do as the Romans failed to do and worship their gods. In the United States, introduce a nice, inoffensive non-sectarian prayer into the public schools. To quote an old Americanism, your religion doesn't matter so long as you've got one.

As the President would say, and did, of prayer: "I don't know of anyone who was hurt by it." It's an attitude that reflects a general lack of interest in anything deep or complex about religion. That attitude has made us a superficial but also a tolerant and peaceful community. Doctrinal differences evaporate and the general assumption permeates that one religion is as good as another. A formal allegiance to a church is assumed, but anything deeper may be suspect. Then people might wonder if you're strange—a Holy Roller, a fanatic, a Christer, a Catholic...

This is scarcely a new American approach, as readers of deTocqueville will recall. Here are his observations on American religion well over a century ago:

"It must never be forgotten that religion gave birth to Anglo-American society. In the United States, religion is therefore mingled with all the habits of the nation and all the feelings of patriotism, whence it derives a particular force.... Christianity has ... retained a strong hold on the public mind in America ... its sway is not only that of a philosophical doctrine which has been adopted upon inquiry, but of a religion which is believed without discussion. In the United States, Christian sects are infinitely diversified and perpetually modified; but Christianity itself is an established and irresistible fact, which no one undertakes either to attack or to defend."

The historian Daniel Boorstin, with his usual acuity, has defined Americanized religion by three characteristics: (1) It is instrumental. That is, it may be valued not for itself but for its uses. The family that prays together stays together, Greece and Rome fell when they abandoned their gods, religion is the secret of success, and so on. (2) It is personal rather than communal: So long as a fellow follows his own faith, even if it's not mine, he's okay. (3) It's non-denominational. What church, if any, does Ronald Reagan belong to, and who cares?

Perhaps the best, quickest, most instinctive summary of this vague but proud allegiance to religion may be found in an offhand comment made by Dwight D. Eisenhower, another nonsectarian: "I am the most intensely religious man I know. That doesn't mean I adhere to any sect. A democracy cannot exist without a religious base. I believe in democracy."

Defending the ancient gods or pushing for school prayers, Mr. Reagan represents not an exception but a kind of unthinking rule, and in one way a salutary rule. Those who don't think very deeply about religion are not inclined to persecute others in its name, even as they try to impress their vague religiosity on others. It's a tossup whether such an attitude is a greater offense against church or state, against those who take religious doctrine to be of transcendental importance, or against those who believe government should have no connection with religion.

Perhaps it was appropriate that this President should have had a good word for the rituals of the ancients. For he reflects an attitude toward religion that the American republic shares with the Roman empire, an attitude Gibbon summarized well enough: "The various modes of worship, which prevailed in the Roman world, were all considered by the people as equally true; by the philosopher, as equally false; and by the magistrate, as equally useful."

Religion in Russia

ZAGORSK, U.S.S.R.—This is the place the guide books say not to miss—the ancient monastery an hour from Moscow, for centuries the focus of pilgrimages and vows, and still the seat of the Russian Orthodox Church. From afar the gold-and-white churches, with their onion-shaped domes and delicate crosses, glisten in the sun, beckoning. The priest who welcomes us is understandably proud as he recites the history of this place and points out the huge ledger containing messages from visiting dignitaries. "Besides visitors from Earth," he beams, "we do have visitors from the Heavens..." He explains that he means the American astronauts who once visited here with their Soviet counterparts.

Our host whisks us through the grounds and in and out of various chapels, some of them full of pilgrims swaying to ancient responses. Leaving one service, he bends down to pick up some of the unconsecrated host from a big wooden box in the foyer. He hands out the biscuits to the visitors as a mid-morning snack.

Here and there, some of the icons have been carefully peeled from the walls, and replaced by replicas. Or their places have been left vacant. They can be seen in the adjoining museum, where thousands of icons have been collected, classified and catalogued. A young expert explains the priceless value of the world-famous collection. As a spiritual center, Zagorsk is a marvelous museum.

Then it is time to meet the heads of the seminary in their black robes and black beards. In their homilies, Brothers Vladimir, Ivan and Alexei Ilich explain that "we are in the first ranks of peace lovers," that peace is the paramount issue in the world for it unites materialism and religion, that Soviet missiles in Europe do not constitute the dangerous threat the new American ones would, that religious dissenters have only themselves to blame for their troubles because they don't adequately support the state, and "the Afghans would have peace if not for aggression from abroad." The last is clearly not meant as a reference to the 100,000 Soviet troops in Afghanistan at the time.

With the exception of the speeches at the Soviet foreign ministry, this has been perhaps the most worldly presentation the visiting editors have heard. At the end, the priests propose to ask the Americans some questions. The first one: "Why do you come here to a religious place and talk only about politics?"

It is Gene Autry Owens, editorial page editor of the *Roanoke Times and World News,* who dubs this troika The Three Stooges, and the name sticks. They are the perfect representatives of Sovreligion, exemplifying what our guides keep telling us is "the separation of church and state in the Soviet Union." That phrase covers a multitude of signs—the absence of religious schools for children, the suppression of religion outside the usual and well-policed channels, and The Three Stooges' clear mastery of the Soviet catechism. When asked how comfortable the church can be in an atheistic society, one of the priests replies, gratefully, "the state gave me what I have now," specifically mentioning his extensive education. The performance might profit any Americans who think it would be a great thing if the government did more to support religion.

According to the litany from our guides, religion in the Soviet Union attracts only old people and a few of the young. The Baptist Church in Moscow attracts enough of the old and young to hold services six nights a week. On the week night one of our group attended, some 600 worshippers showed up. The hymn "What a Friend We Have in Jesus" was readily recognizable when sung in Russian.

The city tour of Novosibirsk stops for twenty minutes on a Sunday morning at the old wooden Church of the Assumption. Inside is the most colorful, the most moving, the most *alive* sight we have seen in grimy Novosibirsk—hundreds of people packed into the old church, the white hair of old men and the bright kerchiefs of women bobbing together as the congregation repeats the responses by heart. The priests in purple vestments lead the standing worshippers. (There are no pews in a Russian Orthodox church; the people stand.) A series of choirs sing out from the balcony. One mass is ending. Then will come a memorial service, a wedding, a funeral.... Scores of people of all ages have been baptized that morning and confessions heard. Our Soviet guides do not linger. (Do they think religion is infectious?)

The people all about us are *praying*—singing and weeping and imploring, being strengthened and strengthening each other. The Intourist bus can damnably well go on without us, doubtless to another statue of Lenin. (Surely no editorial writer who has toured the Soviet Union for three weeks and has seen all those icons of Lenin in every town square, on factory walls, in schools and libraries and meeting halls will ever again casually employ the phrase, godless Communism.)

The priest tells us there are 10,000 baptisms a year in the church, that religion is strong in the surrounding Siberian villages, that it takes 20 priests to meet the needs of 300,000 worshippers in this part of Siberia, that there are also Baptist and Roman Catholic churches in the city. We stay on and on, realizing that we have been starved on this trip not just for fresh fruit and green vegetables but for the spirit, for prayer undisguised and appeals uncalculated.

We're asked where we're from, and are hugged and hugged again. An old nun has taken a liking to red-cheeked Mary Lawrence of the *Indianapolis News* and keeps presenting her with apples, eggs, rolls, the shewbread.... A woman presses an apple on my wife, who has nothing to give her in return except a button that says Arkansas Is a Natural. I pin it on the woman's scarf and she touches it lovingly. We hate to leave. This church—it's definitely not a museum—has ministered not only to its people this day but to some strangers in a strange land.

Walking back to the hotel, we run into a crowd leaving a circus. But we have just seen a greater spectacle, and I bet it will have a longer run.

There are two ways to destroy the religious spirit in man. The first is to oppress and vilify it, and try to reduce it to a matter of bought priests and empty ceremony—to an exhibit in a museum. The second is to make religion semi-official, a sign of respectability and a virtual requirement for worldly success. The first is the Soviet way, and it isn't nearly as effective as the second, the American way.

The Void

Despite all the thousands of words written about Jim and Tammy Fay Bakker, there is a gaping hole in their story: No one has explained their appeal. What is it that managed to propel these two into the first ranks of televangelism? What is missing in American religion that the Bakkers supplied? Is the search for meaning in life so great out there, and so unrewarding, that for millions the void must be filled by simulacra like Jim and Tammy?

The Bakkers' story won't be complete, or perhaps even very significant, until amusement with their misadventures begins to fade and thoughtfulness sets in. When their downfall ceases to be a source of unholy glee, and begins to inspire terror at the emptiness of lives that required their glitzy ministry, then something of substance may yet emerge from this saga—but not before.

What has happened to American religion, and seems to happen to it regularly, that leaves the field open for the Bakkers and all the other variations on an all-too-familiar theme? Why are Americans drawn to the electronic pew the way they once were to tent carnivals? What has produced the religious void these mediaministers fill?

Flannery O'Connor was once asked why Southern authors were always writing about grotesques and misfits. Miss O'Connor replied that Southerners write about freaks because we in this part of the country can still tell a freak when we see one. Can we still? Anybody can spot the grotesques on the church channel, but how many have noticed the transformation of the American church? It is fast becoming a combination social club, welfare agency, bureaucracy, political pressure group, cultural society, and whatever else you'd like instead of a church.

The concept of vocation in the modern world comes to mean something besides a religious one. Jacques Ellul, the French thinker, spotted the trend years ago when he argued that "vocation is under a shadow with Christians due to the fact that the Church's responsible people (pastors, etc.) feel very much debased in a world of technique since they are not themselves specialists, and especially not technicians. To obey a calling and then to preach, to direct a congregation, to take time out for soul-searching—all this seems frivolous in a world of engineers and producers. So, these embarrassed pastors also want to become technicians. They therefore practice psychoanalysis, group dynamics, social psychology, information theory, etc. And it is as psychoanalysts that they will act upon the Christian community—no longer because they were called upon by God for service. Here again it is totally illusory to believe that technique is simply added to, or serves, vocation; technique *in fact* substitutes for vocation." This fashionable trend is scarcely confined to Christians. A critic of the same tendency among Jews once commented that, when rabbis began calling themselves doctors, Judaism grew sick. Increasingly, religion seems as abandoned to the world as anything else in it.

The study of Scripture itself is not immune from the trendy. Paul Minear, the Biblical scholar, put it like this: "Like Americans junketing in Asia, we can carefully select the itinerary, stop only at Western-style hotels, use guides who speak fluent English, eat only American food, albeit with quaint seasonings, and shop for foreign bric-a-brac with Bankamericards. Indeed the guiding of travelers through the world of the Bible with a minimum of culture shock is often assumed to be the chief function of ministers and teachers.... They preserve the illusion of travel, without its risk or its profit. They remain blissfully unaware of how completely they have destroyed the integrity and independence of that other world."

So much effort is expended in making religion effortless, respectable, simple, and, in short, ordinary, that those who have tamed it wonder what more the consumer can want. They may be genuinely mystified when people, in their hunger for the spirit, turn to a television set. "Little does contemporary religion ask of man," the late Abraham Joshua Heschel observed. "Its acceptance involves neither risk nor strain. Religion has achieved respectability by the grace of society..."

There seems to be an immense competition now to offer the cheapest of grace. The vacuum that many find in organized religion drives them to the most disorganized kind. That may explain the attraction of Jim and Tammy Faye and all their host on the small bright tube. None of this is new under the sun, to judge by Jeremiah's ancient plaint: "A wonderful and horrible thing is committed in the land; the prophets prophesy falsely...and my people love to have it so..."

What kind of religious wasteland would give rise to today's phantasmagorical selection of televangelists, one for every taste and disillusion? Because the church must labor in the obdurate world rather than in the television studio, it is tempted to compete by offering a variety of services and appeals that would do justice to a department store. And it may fail all the more.

The immense "success" of the Jim and Tammy Show was a striking measure of what is missing in American lives. The Bakkers' fall will be as empty as their rise if no one asks why people were so drawn to them, and what is so lacking in our lives that we are attracted by this wonderful and horrible thing, and why we love to have it so.

Binx and the Malaise

I heard the news in late May as I was walking into the Sno-White Cafe here in Pine Bluff, Ark.

Walker Percy died, Roger Coley told me. Roger is a Mississippi boy who's now design editor at the *Pine Bluff Commercial*. Newspapers have titles like Design Editor these days. He stopped in front of the dusty door to tell me. I walked right in, even managed to order a cheeseburger uptown—that's with tomato, lettuce, and mayonnaise—but I was stunned. I didn't know what to say. We talked about the weather.

A drenching-wet spring was turning into the kind of dry-as-dust summer that I used to revel in when I was younger. On the first really hot hot day in Pine Bluff, when the heat turns every metal surface into a grill, and bounces off walls like it'll never stop, I used to make a point of wandering through the warehouse district a couple of blocks away around Third and Alabama, just to feel the summer returning like a Southern childhood, coming on like the world everlasting. I'm not quite up to that any more, not after a sunstroke a few years ago, but the return of unbearable summer still fills me with unreasonable joy. I have a friend who on the first night when the heat won't stop no matter how late makes a point of driving out in the country along Bayou Bartholomew with his air conditioning going full blast but all the car windows down, so he can both survive and breathe in the absolute rankness of spring utterly undone by summer as the bugs splatter on the windshield. If Herbert W. Armstrong is on the radio with news of *The Wo-orld Tomorrow,* it's the epitome of South. I guess everybody has his own ritual, his own sign and wonder. It's like the rainbow given to Noah and his crew, an assurance that the cycle goes on and on. And then I hear Walker Percy is dead.

I knew he was sick—I heard he resigned from the LSU board of trustees or some such awhile back for reasons of health. But you're never prepared, never, for something like that. You hear about it and you realize the minute hand of your own life has slipped forward and, though nothing has changed outwardly, everything's different inwardly. The scenery shrivels and the colors change; it's not the same without him here to see it.

I have to tell you I was hurt nobody told me any sooner. Here in Arkansas we're always treated like poor relations. I had read about the death of modernist playwrights and ex-governors and such in the public prints, but there was nary a mention of Walker Percy that I saw. His obituary in the *New York Times* must have been in one of those that stack up before I can get to it. I felt like an old and not very suitable beau that the bride's family sends a wedding invitation on the day of the ceremony—so they'll be sure he won't show up and embarrass everybody. It's not the same, celebrating—or mourning—out of sync with everybody else. It's a kind of chronological alienation. It lends perspective, all right, which is just what the modern world has too much of now. You can't take it as hard as you want to, seeing how it's a week or two past. Yet it's news to *you*. You don't know how to behave, except in the most polite, acceptable way.

Me, I ate my cheeseburger and kept talking, talking to poor Roger about *The Moviegoer,* Walker Percy's first book, and how much it meant to me at the time. That must have been about 1962, when I was between jobs and careers and women and cities. *The Moviegoer* does more than stand up on rereading; it changes every time, or at least my reaction does. Come to think, that's just why Binx Bolling, its hero—well, protagonist—keeps going to old movies: not because they change but because he's changed enough for them to tell him something different. The same chinaberries may be crushed against the same sidewalks outside more and more remote neighborhood theaters, but the movie itself hasn't changed. It's the one standard measurement—like the golden yardstick you hear about somewhere in the federal vaults—by which everything else can be measured. I guess movies were ol' Binx's first day of real summer. He kept coming back to them to escape what he called the Malaise.

Malaise used to be a good word before Jimmy Carter ruined it, and a lot better than the literary equivalent, Anomie. Malaise was just the right word *circa* 1962, when *The Moviegoer* was first published. Now

the politicians have absconded with the word. Binx was much afflicted
with it. Malaise didn't make him evil or sinful. The beauty of Binx is
that there was nothing unique about him, including his incapacity to
do anything as meaningful, as human, as to sin. That's what terrified
him, the absence of terror. Walker Percy had that just right.

Malaise: I remember how Walker Percy had Binx describe it that
evening in Gentilly back in the early sixties, when the buildings were
low against the sky and deserted at the end of the day, and the
occasional gas station attendants hosed down the concrete under their
"glowing discs and shells and stars." For once and ever the reader saw
the beauty and transience and ordinariness of it, and the emptiness of
our distractions:

> On the way home, I stop off at the Tivoli. It is a Jane Powell picture
> and I have no intention of seeing it. However, Mr. Kinsella the
> manager sees me and actually pulls me in by the coatsleeve for a
> sample look. He says it is a real pleaser and he means it. There go
> Jane and some fellow walking arm in arm down the street in a high
> wide and handsome style and doing a wake up and sing number.
> The doorman, the cop on the corner, the taxi driver, each sunk in
> his own private misery, smile and begin to tap their feet. I am hardly
> ever depressed by a movie and Jane Powell is a very nice-looking
> girl, but the despair of it is enough to leave you gone in the
> stomach.

God, isn't that the truth? What Binx wanted, what we want, is
some relief from the Malaise, and recognizing it is the first step.
Walker Percy didn't just name it, the way some textbook on Existentialism
101 would, complete with index, genealogy, and required reading, but
he made blank art of it, as close and as distant as New Orleens Land of
Dreems. Reading *The Moviegoer* made you want to drive down to
Metairie *right now* just to see what wasn't there, till you snapped to
and realized you might as well stay where you were, 'cause it wasn't
here, either.

In Walker Percy, the post-sixties at last got our counterpoint to
Faulkner—the Dixie Express, Flannery O'Connor called him. And
the roar and rumble of him was so great and thick and all-encompassing

when he went by that nothing but it existed, and we just can't live immersed in all that all the time. Besides, everything was changing, as it always does, and who would record this different South, or even non-South?

Damn it, Faulkner has become part of the Malaise, too. He has become the great backdrop against which those who come after have to carry on, play our parts, recite our lines, live our scripted lives long after the whole theater has crumbled around us. José Ortega y Gasset says somewhere that culture is a series of swimming strokes amidst the continuous shipwreck that is life. (I guess not knowing life is shipwreck is Malaise.) The strokes keep us afloat, but once the seas calm they're no longer necessary. We keep practicing them anyway, and making sure the successive generations learn them ever so exactly, not realizing that they have become ornamental rather than necessary—Culture rather than culture. You can sense it happening to Faulkner even if I'll be damned rather than admit it.

A great artist is a great inner tyrant; he can't help but dictate. Some of the devotees read through the Faulknerian canon every year, the way churches go through the Bible. Is it possible to do that and lead one's own life? Isn't it mesmerizing and exhausting enough just to read *Light in August* every December, in time for Christmas? To study Scripture, a wise rabbi once told me, one has to know how to do two things: to enter and to emerge. The entering is the easy part, the irresistible part. But how emerge? And what is left when one does? A sense of loss. The Malaise.

Faulkner crystallized that sense of loss forever in his world squeezed into a sentence, his inexhaustible world carved in interminable sentences, and so deprived us of our own sense of loss. But Walker Percy emerged out of Mississippi (of course) and restored it to us—a whole different sense of loss, ineffable and inexplicable but unmistakable. A *recognized* emptiness, even if there was the danger of feeling it too strongly, of sentimentalizing it. In our rapture with *The Moviegoer,* we were reduced to talking in italicized prose—like one of Walker Percy's less appealing characters. Our enthusiasm knew no boundaries or articulation. We loved Binx as surely as we loved, or hated, or despaired of ourselves. He had that wonderful, almost unaware sense of *vacancy* that still waits for us at every turn. The specific character of despair, Kierkegaard said, is precisely this: It is unaware of being despair.

There were moments, just moments, when John Bickerson Bolling of Metairie, La., did grow aware, when he beat the Malaise, even if he didn't think he had. For example on page 99 of my edition of *The Moviegoer*:

> For some time now the impression has been growing upon me that everyone is dead. It happens when I speak to people. In the middle of a sentence it will come over me; yes, beyond a doubt, this is death. There is little to do but groan and make an excuse and slip away as quickly as one can. At such times it seems that the conversation is spoken by automatons who have no choice in what they say. I hear myself or someone else saying things like: "In my opinion the Russian people are a great people, but—" or "Yes, what you say about the hypocrisy of the North is unquestionably true. However—" and I think to myself: this is death. Lately it is all I can do to carry on such everyday conversations, because my cheek has developed a tendency to twitch of its own accord. Wednesday as I stood speaking to Eddie Lovell, I felt my eye closing in a broad wink.

Haven't you had that feeling? Don't you even now? Would you believe that in the middle of some board meeting or press conference or lovely occasion, it is all I can do to resist standing up and saying in a loud voice: "Do you know all of us are going to die?" I hold back; I don't want to be thought some kind of fanatic. But my soul thirsts. I can hear it panting. I keep running across the kind of phrase that caught Binx's attention ("... hopefully awaiting the gradual convergence of the physical sciences and the social sciences") and that left him abandoned on the endless plateau of Malaise. Do you have any idea how many times a day an editorial page editor sees phrases like that?

I always liked sportswriters, but used to think of myself as a cut above. How many synonyms can you think of for Win, Lose, or Tie? How many ways to tell the same story, even if the names and stadia are different? But of late it's hit me. Political commentary is an unchanging game, too. Only the names change. How many synonyms are there for Win, Lose, Tie, and *hubris*? For just a blessed moment—I think it's blessed—one becomes aware of the Malaise, which may be the only way to overcome it.

It wasn't the same reading Walker Percy after *The Moviegoer,* though there were flashes in his other books. The desperate questions he raised were so much better than any of his wise answers. The Malaise has all the answers; it's the questions that still rouse and return us to life. That's why I'll keep reading *The Moviegoer.*

Baal, Ashtaroth, and Self-Esteem

Some of us thought the market for the newest psychological wonder drug, Self-Esteem, was limited to the more laid-back parts of California. We were wrong. A joint legislative committee in Arkansas, outpost of biblical language and the work ethic, has just heard a solemn proposal to finance a state Task Force on Self-Esteem and Personal and Social Responsibility. Arkansas should be making Doonesbury any day now.

When this kind of psychobabble can be taken seriously by legislators in a populist, independent, not to say just-plain-contrary state like good ol' Arkinsaw, you know the whole country has to be inundated with junk thought.

Listen to Representative Pat Flanigan of Forrest City on the need for a statewide task force (committees are now invariably called task forces) on S-E and P-and-SR: "It's not a panacea, but it's a starting point."

Well, he's half right. It's definitely no panacea. But self-esteem is not a starting point, either. If it's anything like what used to be called self-respect, it's a finishing point—because self-esteem must be grounded in achievement and backed by faith. In theological terms, which acquire an increasingly quaint sound in this biblically illiterate society, self-esteem grows out of both works and grace. They have a way of going together.

Of course nobody in the self-esteem industry would be caught speaking of works and grace. Like so much else in the modern world, the self-esteem fad is one more attempt to find an acceptably secular substitute for religious values. Hence the tinny sound of the vocabulary in which it is offered.

"An indestructible sense of self-worth," Professor Paula Prentiss told this committee, "cannot be bought. It must be modeled." She is a professor of education. You can tell by the language. It's called Educanto, and consists of equal parts hubris, hollowness and human engineering.

It doesn't take a task force to discover the obvious. Here are some ways to build self-esteem, not just in schools:

—Train people to be independent.

—Have students learn solid skills: how to read, write and cipher.

—Encourage people to appreciate things of use and beauty, as opposed to platitudes.

—Treat others with respect. That includes expecting competence, and not pretending it's there when it ain't. The latter may be the cruelest hoax perpetrated on today's students—also on today's consumers and taxpayers. Get rid of frauds like social promotion, meaningless diplomas and undergraduate schools of education. Have teachers get an education before they start taking "education" courses that are all form and no content.

—Raise standards, don't lower them.

—Let the honor of others be as dear to us as our own. Start with manners. ("Sir. Ma'am. Thank you. You're welcome. I'm sorry. May I help you?")

—Tolerate people, not shoddy performance or foggy thought. And don't just tolerate differences; relish them.

Finally, could we please stop blaming the public schools for every defect of society and everything else that may irritate us? The schools have become a kind of receiver-in-bankruptcy for the family, the church and society. It doesn't do much for their self-esteem.

Is there a problem that other institutions have failed to solve? Then saddle the schools with it and fill up the curriculum with unending frills like self-esteem. When the schools can no longer find the time or resources to teach the fundamentals, express shock and dismay. That is a formula for failure.

All of this assumes that the word Self-Esteem has meaning. It may not. By the time junk thought arrives in Arkansas from California or New York, it may be on its last, transparent legs. Fadtalk has a remarkably short shelf life. My state could wind up adopting institutionalized, mass produced, prefabricated Self-Esteem just when the rest of the country has seen through it and is moving on to the next verbal tic. There are many advantages of being this far down in the fashion chain, but one of the disadvantages is a tendency to adopt trends just as they cease to be trends.

What would this Task Force with its 17 members and paid staff of three do? Nothing exactly, to judge by a description in a news dispatch out of Little Rock: "The task force's purpose would be to promote public awareness, keep abreast of new research, monitor the results of area task forces and basically try to integrate an understanding of the importance of self-esteem throughout government and free enterprise."

Blah blah, blah blah, blah *blah*. Does such a specimen of Educanto *mean* anything? Empty language is the surest sign of weak ideas, and maybe a lack of self-esteem.

Speaking up for yuppiedom's latest, psychologically approved fad, Arkansas's attorney general put in a plug for teaching self-esteem in the schools. "Until we get our young people to feeling good about themselves with positive attitudes," said Winston Bryant, slipping into his Norman Vincent Peale mode, "then I don't think our education system will work very well..."

General Bryant's approach to the question of how to build self-esteem, formerly known as self-respect, can be summed up simply enough: First get a cart, then put it before the horse. Just feel good and achievement will follow. This isn't just instant gratification; it's pre-gratification. So much for the work ethic, which is a second cousin to the Protestant Ethic. In today's with-it psychology, that kind of Calvinist heresy is strictly taboo.

With timid educators confusing the separation of church and state with that of religion and life, it would be risky to let innocent schoolchildren in on the old theory that we're all children of God— and made in His image. How's that for self-esteem? Much better to leave that kind of psychotherapy alone. It's dynamite.

It might also be considered hopelessly old-fashioned to quote Abe Lincoln on the subject: "It is difficult to make a man miserable while he feels he is worthy of himself and claims kindred to the great God who made him." Now *that's* self-esteem. Or maybe grace.

Is it unconstitutional to expose the young to such thoughts, but lawful to introduce them to the First Church of Feelgood, a kind of secular religion right down to its rigid intolerance for heresies?

It can all be pretty confusing when you think about it. But of course the trick is not to think about it, but just go along with every new fad out of the educationists' ever-busy fudge factory. That's why they speak in Educanto; the lingo makes thought unnecessary. Like Newspeak in *1984,* it's a language designed not only to avoid other kinds of communication but to make them impossible. Once the old words are abolished and replaced with Newspeak, how describe concepts like grace, salvation, works, soul? Instead, one is reduced to repeating in-words like self-esteem.

If it is wrong for the public schools to usurp the role of home and church, and impose religion on children—and it is—then why is it right for the schools to preach or practice a latter-day, watered-down, dumbed-down, psyched-up secularized substitute for religion so dim it isn't cognizant that it's a form of religion, namely, self-worship? The self-esteemers seem blissfully unaware of their own philosophical underpinnings, weak as those are. Heaven help us, modern language is so dull and confused that even our abominations are no longer intelligible. At least Baal and Ashtaroth offered something definite, like good crops. Self-esteem is to faith as New Age music is to Bach.

It is a common misconception that America has no established religion. In this era, it's the same one that dominated Rome, paganism. And while that creed may be established only informally, it is all the more influential for not being limited to formal confines. It can be all-pervasive.

Just flip through the channels on your television set for a comprehensive kaleidoscope of the separate but equal god of your choice: the business of sport or the sport of business; any variety of lust, violence and corruption an ambitious screenwriter can merchandise; news as entertainment and entertainment as news; opinion as analysis and analysis as opinion; tag-team shouting matches billed as political debate; materialism in your choice of colors or in simple, classic black-and-white; the futuristic or nostalgic, depending on your taste and mood; Bill Moyers or Elm Street's Jason Voorhees; Alistair Cooke or Arsenio Hall; Pat Robertson or Pat Paulsen; the War Between the States in the latest and most acceptable historiography or good old *Gone With the Wind*; docudramas and sitcoms, though it's not always easy to distinguish between them; wars and rumors of wars; three-minute hates or love, both alchemized into sentimentality; faith made kitsch and kitsch considered art. . . . and self-esteem, of course.

Mix and match, pick and choose, and no mere Roman pantheon was ever so electronically variegated. It's not just Bach that's synthesized in our age but Walt Whitman. And now our children can have self-esteem thanks to a state commission.

Awe and trembling, works and grace, all can be overcome, or just put aside, and the self will be elevated to its rightful, esteemed place. There will no longer be old doubts in this new, multi-screen heaven and earth, let alone any need for the old assurances. The economy will rebound, jobs multiply, and children achieve. The only sin will be the sense of sin, the only forbidden activity introspection, the only heresy solitude, the only music missing that of blessed silence. And if that still small voice can nevertheless be heard, just turn up the volume and drown it out.

Should this brave new world only depress, fear not. The psychologically with-it will teach us self-esteem. They will save us, though we be not saved. They will heal us, though we be not healed.

Inerrancy at Bobby Joe's

By the time Ashley Gurney, Esq., made it over to Bobby Joe's Cafe and Radiator Shoppe, the lunchtime crowd had thinned out but the place was still full of dirty dishes, leftover talk, and day-old fellowship. As he eased his not inconsiderable bulk onto one of the stools that still had all its vinyl, Counselor Gurney noticed a single, solitary figure down at the other end of the lunch counter, where an aura of contemplation had settled in.

Then again, maybe it was just the cigarette smoke or perfume. Some of the sales ladies from the Bon-Ton had started frequenting the place, probably on a dare. Soon they'd be painting the walls and putting up posters of French impressionists. How long before the toothpicks disappeared, the formica dinette tables outnumbered the vinyl booths, and all the dishes matched? Ashley Gurney silently resolved to take his custom elsewhere as soon as he spotted the first fern.

"What's the matter with our friend?" he asked when Cleola finally asked for his order.

"Oh, Jimmy Lee," she said. "No tellin'. Usually he's frisky as a colt. He come in here today and didn't want nothin' but water and a dish of greens. And him already so thin he don't have but one side. I don't know if his wife ran off with his best friend or what, but he looks like his heart's as heavy as a bucket of hog livers. Usually he's happy as a tick on a deer. He's been sittin' there for an hour meditatin'. What'll it be—Mr. Ashley, the usual with pickled okra?"

"No, I'm cuttin' down, Cleola. Just a little of the three-bean salad and a biscuit. Well, maybe a corndog for protein. And a chili pie—but a small one. Cream gravy on the side. Hold the brown derby cone today. And iced tea—I'll take it with Jimmy Lee. Looks like he could use some comfortin', and I haven't had a divorce case in a while. Maybe we can get the wife for alienation of affection."

Ashley Gurney eased himself within range of Jimmie Lee Smitherman's

palpable angst, and adopted his Concerned, Ever-Ready-to-Help
look, which most people confused with a squint.

"Got something in your eye?" asked Jimmie Lee, breaking out of
his distraction long enough to notice the oncoming lawyer.

"I just noticed you down here, Jimmie Lee. You look stuck between
a brown study and a blue funk. I'd call it a beige haze. Can I help?"

"I don't think so," said Jimmie Lee in absent-minded candor,
shifting his gaze back to the bottle of Tabasco sauce he'd been
studying. "It's a religious thing. I been reading and thinking and
listening to all them het-up preachers, and I done read every Baptist
newsletter I get on the subject, and I'm afraid when I get to them
pearly gates, the first question old Saint Pete is goin' to ask is if I
believe in itinerancy or not and I won't know what to say…"

"Inerrancy," corrected Ashley Gurney, his features relaxing into his
usual, not unfriendly scowl. He himself was a lapsed Presbyterian
who favored the Episcopal church for aesthetic reasons. Nevertheless,
he kept up with new trends in theology the way a collector noted the
prices of paintings that no longer fascinated him. "The inerrancy of
the Bible."

"Yeah, that's it. I get confused. It ain't like I got a photogenic
memory and can get all these new words right. They never taught us
that one in Sunday School. They just stuck to the simple stuff—love,
grace, charity, forgiveness, Jesus. We never got to the important stuff
and now I'm lost. I can't even pronounce it, let alone fight over it. I'm
afraid I'm a spiritual failure. My prayer life never prepared me for this
kind of thing. I done met the devil and I'm afraid he's me."

"*Photographic* memory. But don't you believe in the Bible?"

"That ain't enough any more. Now you got to have the votes at the
convention or go off and form your own denomination. Which is the
true church and which the devil's snare? I suppose both could be. It
was hard enough deciding between sprinkling and immersion. Now
we're supposed to take sides between the errant and inerrant, which is
easy enough to do, but ain't nobody admitting to be errant.

"The more I hear," continued Jimmie Lee, "the less I know. I'm
supposed to know who should control the mission money and the
Baptist Press and Baylor University—and I can't even work up an

interest in their football team. I don't know if we got a church any more or a take-over bid. I ain't been so confused since the company I worked for merged and the stock either doubled or disappeared. I ain't sure to this day. I thought I belonged to a church, not a corporation. I just wish we could go back to the Bible stories and listen to 'em the way we did when I was just knee-high to the preacher, but I know that's not enough now."

"Actually, I think yours is quite a sound position, Christologically speaking," said Mr. Gurney between bites of corndog.

"How can that be when I ain't got a position?" asked Jimmie Lee Smitherman, not bothering to transfer his gaze from the small print on the Tabasco bottle. New Iberia, Louisiana, had started to sound like a simple, clear and fascinating place compared to this conversation.

Ashley Gurney, Esq., sighed. He chewed his chili pie, which was slightly singed around the edges, and wished he had some jalapeno peppers to go with it. A stray Bible verse ran through his well ordered mind like a dapple of sunlight along the dusty row of the Annotated Statutes in his office—*Suffer the little children to come unto me, and forbid them not; for of such is the kingdom of God.* Then came the vague remembrance of something he'd read in an unfashionable little theological journal he still subscribed to, mainly for amusement. "Christians are so deeply imbued with the fundamental doctrines of the world that they no longer have any liberty of thought or life." Was that from Jacques Ellul? Anyway, it was surely an exaggeration. You can't have a church without doctrinal disputes any more than you can a society without law—it's a necessary evil.

"I just want to do whatever's fair," Jimmie Lee was saying as he put down the bottle of Tabasco sauce. "Only I don't know what fair is. I tell you, Brother Gurney, all this education about itinerancy has done for me is make me more confused than average."

Ashley Gurney, Esq., was not at all confused but, as he considered a small helping of gooseberry cobbler, he realized he was rather envious of Jimmie Lee Smitherman.

III | THE WRITER

On the Beach

SANTA ROSA ISLAND, Florida—The breakers are two to four feet high. The seawater temperature is in the 60s. High tide is at 9:16 A.M., low tide at 11:30 P.M. Westerly winds at 10 to 15 knots. The highs are in the low 90s, the lows in the 70s. Seaweed is thick. Sunrise is at 5:49 A.M., sunset at 7:55 P.M.

On my lap is an unopened copy of *Public Opinion* by Walter Lippmann, copyright 1922—a piece of salvage acquired on the mainland while casting about secondhand bookstores to see what sea changes might have been made in long familiar standards. One remembers the book as being earnest and sophisticated in the way of the intellectuals of 1920s—before the 1930s knocked the stuffings out of them and just about everybody else. The book was terribly liberal back then, with overtones of government of the few, by the better informed and for the undiscerning many.

But the book stays closed, as it has for so long. It can't compete with the waves, each and every one unique, as always. (How did He manage that one?) The waves come on unceasingly, each at its own pace, and time stops, or ceases to matter. The sound of the cool green surf rises above and apart from the far-seeing calculations of those who would shape Public Opinion, with about as much chance as shaping a wave.

I feel the need to go inside and write something, anything, even a postcard. There are those types who can't go anywhere without taking snapshots. It's the way they validate experience. They get so busy validating they may miss the experience. The pictures become more real than reality. Like the grandmother who is complimented on the grandson she's proudly wheeling around in the stroller—"Oh," she says, "you should see his picture!" The writer has his own version of the Kodak Syndrome. If the experience isn't written down, did it really happen?

Writing it down makes it intelligible, permanent, unchanging. None of which describes reality, despite the illusion of words having captured it. Reality preserved is a contradiction in terms. The words are not the experience any more than the snapshot is. What is fine language anyway but the fabrication of future cliches? These words before you are not what happens on the beach. There is none of the murmuring undulation of the waves in them, the serenity of the shoreline imperceptibly but surely changing with every wash of a wave, no ceaseless sound of the surf even when it cannot be seen in the cool of midnight, none of the pressure of the sunheat beating down and radiating out as though it will not, cannot stop, but has always been just like this. And always will be.

But reality is not in those words, either. The words are only some addictive, delusionary validation of common feelings. But to some of us they become preferable to the experience itself—just as we hurry in off the street and away from the world to visit museums. Those who can, live. Those who can't, make pictures, or jot down endless disconnected notes. Maybe I've been out in the sun too long.

Or maybe it's just the workings of insecurity. Like the fellow who jogs every day because he fears that if he misses just one morning, he'll never run another step. He's propelled forward not by love or challenge, or even by some fool idea of fending off the inevitable and extending life forever, but out of simple desperation. It is anxiety made habitual, which is one description of the human condition. My wife glares at me when she sees me pick up a pencil; I'm supposed to be on vacation.

Imagine a compulsive writer who can take a vacation from writing.

He'd be like a drunk who can lay off the stuff for precisely two weeks before taking it up again on schedule. Or a politician ceasing to think of power for 14 days. Hard to imagine. Why, each one must wonder, do the others do it? What attraction is there in such an addiction? Surely the best kept secret of journalism is the insignificance of its subject.

Maybe what I need is a chapter of Writers Anonymous. But they say one must want to change for that kind of reform to work and, on a day like this, when it's too hot to think, I would rather just go on writing. Thinking is for editors in air-conditioned rooms, for neat types given to pruning kudzuvine. Right now it is too hot to link words in spurious logic, to bother with grammar and syntax and all that goes into fashioning the outward appearance of sense out of the lava flow of words on the beach. Editing is for later, like changing one's ways.

The finished product, after all the fine touches that are such bad ideas, stands like the elaborate sand castle down the way that took the better part of an afternoon to construct in all its transient glory. But those who built it had no illusions of permanence; theirs was an elaborate gesture to the passing moment, an illusion built without illusions. Theirs was an honorable and realistic undertaking compared to writing consciously for posterity.

This morning, running down a road along the beach, I came across a modest, stenciled street sign near some beach cottages. Arkansas Street, it said. Home away from home. I almost tripped over what it had replaced—a stone pillar, its concrete base uprooted and its message half covered by sand and the sea shells they use for gravel around here. "This street," it read, after I had brushed off the words, "This street is dedicated in honor of the State of ARKANSAS Admitted to the Union 1836 This plaque dedicated by Governor ORVAL E. FAUBUS 1965." It scarcely matters now whether it was Camille or Frederick that turned over the pillar, or the more ordinary malice of time. It is still a monument of a kind, like Walter Lippmann's dusty, unread words. In the end they both pay tribute to a different reality, one without pretensions to permanence that nevertheless goes on and on, like the drifting sand and the unceasing waves.

The Wave and the Rock

OGUNQUIT, Maine—I'm here for a convention of the New England Society of Newspaper Editors, who are meeting together with the inky wretches who write their editorials. The company is good but the scenery is spectacular. Between seminars and speeches, I get to watch the waves strike the rocks at Bald Head Cliff, always the same, always different, rinsing the mind. That is the high point of the trip. The rest is journalism.

It's a wonderful thing to have a friend with whom one disagrees completely. She's an editorial writer for a big-city newspaper, which may explain our differences. Her presentation to a group of editorial writers is driven by demographics; she seems as concerned about attracting baby-boomers as I am about keeping the language weeded.

She suggests typographical devices to clarify editorials; I must seem obsessed by the search for just the right word, however elusive.

My friend explains that the two-job family doesn't have time for a leisurely read; I remain convinced that anyone will read an editorial if it's irresistibly written. (I wonder: Did the one-job family have any more time for newspapers? Infants and small children were not known for their patience even in the old days, and households never ran themselves.)

My friend would give people editorials on the subjects the polls say they're interested in. I believe people will read about China or Saturn or even the federal budget if the words are compelling. My theory is that the most insignificant thing about journalism is the subject; what counts is how it's covered.

My friend's emphasis is on how to save the reader time; mine is on how to make the reader want to spend it reading editorials. People do seem to find the time to do what really interests them, whether it's watching the World Series every year, going deer hunting or, yes, reading the paper. The challenge to editors is to make that last activity a must.

It would be unfair to say that my friend is uninterested in good writing, just as it would be unfair to say that I am uninterested in graphics and design. But our philosophies differ markedly. The organizers of the meeting could not have come up with a better contrast. We two meet like the wave and the rock.

My friend would give the reader a simple guide to every editorial, boiling it down, and breaking it into easy-to-digest segments. I ask if she would provide such a guide to the articles by the renowned crime reporter for her paper, whose work is a continuing delight and delicious horror. It is a rhetorical question. No good editor would mess with art. And that's what editorials should be, even if they seldom are.

Reviewing one New England paper's editorials, I want to cry. Not because they are so bad but because they have so many good qualities—labor, conscientiousness, professionalism—and all of them are wasted without art. They're so professional that they lack the essence of an editorial, opinionation. There is no distinctive voice here. This editorial column sounds like a machine rather than a human presence.

An editorial can and should be many things day to day: a spectacle, a meditation, an outburst, the verbal equivalent of a quiet cup of coffee or a stiff drink, a talk with a friend, a lecture from a Dutch uncle, but it ought to be an experience, not a duty, to read. An editorial can be fact-driven or emotion-driven, but too many sound as though they were driven only by the need to fill a certain amount of space every day. It would be a kindness to the reader in such cases to leave the space blank, perhaps adorned with a simple message like: "Compliments of a Friend."

One of the editors said that what he looks for in a newspaper is something that will open the reader's eyes and leave him saying: "Wow!" What does it for him, he confided, was the use of bullets. He means the little typographical gizmos that often separate different points of an article. I asked him to repeat that, to make certain I had heard him correctly. I had.

•

•

•

They don't do a thing for me. I envy him.

Give me words. The kind that pound on the conscience, crack open mysteries, let light shine, or undulate across the page until the reader is hypnotized. I've noticed that when people watch the most graphic of media—television—they keep the sound on, so they can hear the *words*.

Give me words that soothe or alarm, inform or galvanize, open starry skies or peer into hidden recesses. The right words in the right context are like the discrete droplets that rise for a perfect instant when a great wave strikes solid rock. They're fresh as now, old as the world everlasting. Wow. They rinse the mind.

An Exchange on the Language

Paul Greenberg:

I usually admire your column when the *Chicago Tribune* uses it. But your piece on newspapermen and the CIA is unbearably sexist. Aren't you aware that journalism is not a single-sex occupation? Surely as fine a writer as you should be aware of the implications of the words you use and should have command of non-sexist synonyms such as journalist, reporter, and correspondent.

The time is long past when male writers can excuse such careless (or deliberate) sexism by saying "-man" words include women. They don't. Historically, they haven't. And they are still part of a mindset that makes it easy not even to think about the possibility that women could do such jobs.

Joan Beck
Chicago Tribune

Dear, Dear Joan Beck,
 Peace.
 I am sorry if I offended you, but I cannot say I am sorry if I offended against some idea that the English language must be cut and trimmed to fit the ideological pressures of the moment. I realize that Webster's need not be the last word on the subject, but its definition of newspaperman does not seem bound by gender: "a person regularly employed as a writer or editor on the editorial staff of a newspaper or news agency." That is the way I intended the term and if Mr. Webster's support is not sufficient grounds for acquittal, at least I hope it would entitle me to a fair trial rather than an automatic verdict of guilty on the charge of sexism.
 If I must avoid all such terms in the future, does this mean that henceforth I am barred from referring to Flannery O'Connor, Janet Flanner, or Mary McCarthy as craftsmen? Must I find "non-sexist synonyms" for that perfectly good word, too? Like artificer, or artisan, or wright? But they no more satisfy than journalist, reporter, or correspondent in place of newspaperman. The best definition of journalist I have heard didn't come from Webster's: A journalist is someone who borrows ten bucks from a newspaperman and forgets to return it. Really, wouldn't you rather be a newspaperwoman—even at the risk of the whole class being known as newspapermen—than a journalist? Or, even worse, a member of that impersonal glob, The Media?
 If I had not meant to refer to newspapermen—with that word's virile and, yes, muliebral connotations of clacking typewriters, crowded city rooms and a general lack of airs—then I would have used another word. To me, journalist has the sound of somebody who writes for quarterlies and wouldn't know a galley from a ukulele. If I used the wrong word, it was not without thought or in order to exclude women from the club.

For a happy instant, I entertained the thought that you were making a conscious joke when you wrote: "The time is long past when male writers can excuse such careless (or deliberate) sexism by saying 'man' words include women." Must woman, too, be censored from the language? I hope not; I am even more fond of women than of newspapermen, and refuse to give up that word in exchange for some unsatisfactory substitute like female, lady (a much diluted term in any case these days), or dame. Except of course where appropriate. Wouldn't you rather be identified as a woman, rather than an androgynous person? (Except perhaps on those occasions when you want to melt into the crowd.)

Admittedly, the fun of language—and of this exchange—lies in tumult and change, not stasis. But surely that doesn't mean we must censor good, old, distinguishing words because they fail to meet some ideological test and substitute a "non-sexist" Newspeak for language. One of the glories of the English tongue, it was once understood, is its wealth of vocabulary—with each word boasting its own shade of meaning, rhythm, sound, and satisfying use.

Our difference in this matter may have to do with more than individual words, or even whole classes of words; it reflects the old tension between language and politics. Tyrants long have recognized the utility of compressing language to fit their own ideological mold, and the do-gooders probably joined them shortly thereafter. Indeed, it is not always easy to discern one group from the other. For those who corrupt language may soon enough find that they have corrupted themselves. The new wordsmiths may be making the same old error, assuming that if only the ends are justified, then so are the means. In this case, they would equate words of different connotations, or censor selected words in order to stamp out a subversive "mindset."

I am not at all sure if the mentality of a culture—its mindset, if you will—can be altered so easily. For which I am grateful. See how even totalitarian societies may have difficulty making their subjects swallow an endless stream of propaganda. But even if some good could be done that way, I would not sacrifice a single slight shade of meaning nor a singular old word or phrase, in order to gain some transient social or political end. For even if the rights of a whole group could be obtained in that fashion, what would those rights be worth in a society in which words and the ideas they represent—including the concepts of equal rights and equal opportunity—could be so readily manipulated?

Forgive me for carrying on so about words. But I think they are important. They may be the most important thing we've got and we need to hold on to them for dear life, words being the life of thought.

Yours truly,
Paul Greenberg

Writing and Thinking

The boy called home the other evening from Washington, where he has a summer job that involves some writing and editing. He mentioned that he'd heard Adam Meyerson, editor of *Policy Review*, comment that most writers hated writing. That brings to mind Red Smith's old observation that writing is easy—all you have to do is sit down at a typewriter and open a vein. The boy asked if I felt that way, and I said, "No, I enjoy it. The hard part is the thinking. The best part is after you've got the first draft done and you can concentrate on the writing, the polishing."

After he'd hung up, I realized I had fallen into the oldest fallacy about writing—the assumption that there is a clear distinction between writing and thinking, the word and the thought, and once you've thought about something (wordlessly, somehow) you sit down and perform the mechanical task of putting it on paper. 'Tain't so. Words are thought—its coinage and instrument and test and, yes, thought itself. That may be why writers are so often tongue-tied; we keep rearranging sentences even as we speak them, thinking them through again. Thought and its expression are part of the same process; writing *is* thinking.

Maybe that's also why ghostwriters tend to prove unsatisfying. The politician or business executive who comes up with a Great Thought but just needs somebody to "put it into words" may be disappointed when it doesn't sound as good as he imagined it; it has failed the test of language, which is the best test of thought. The good ghostwriter must know not only language but how his client thinks. Unless he knows that, the ghostwritten speech will usually sound like a ghostwritten speech. It will lack the personal touch, or at least the personal touch of the speaker. When a ghostwritten speech sparkles, it may be with another's charm, as if the speaker had gone out and bought not only a new suit for the occasion but a new personality.

What makes writing difficult is that it involves thought, and thinking is work. Yet there is never a shortage of people who want to write. There must be almost as many frustrated writers in the world as there are frustrated politicians. H. L. Mencken once explained that writing for a living was a kind of personality disorder. His theory was that "an author, like any other so-called artist, is a man in whom the normal vanity of all men is so vastly exaggerated that he finds it a sheer impossibility to hold it in. His overpowering impulse is to gyrate before his fellow men, flapping his wings and emitting defiant yells. This being forbidden by the police of all civilized countries, he takes it out by putting his yells on paper. Such is the thing called self-expression."

The enduring charm of Mr. Mencken's work can be explained by his ability to transform that original impulse into words that make sense and feeling—even after half a century. The first steps in the writing process may be painful as one watches what seemed a great idea fail the test of words, or turn into something entirely different. But it is satisfying to watch something of form and substance emerge from the inchoate mass. When it's done well, the writer feels like a sculptor chiseling away deftly at a block of stone. If done poorly day after day, stroke after stroke, the effect on both writer and reader is more like that of the Chinese water torture.

If the form that emerges is misshapen and without substance, the sense of defeat is total, and the only saving hope is that some editor with good sense will crumple up the product and see that it lands in the wastebasket instead of in print. The great service of editors is to save writers immense embarrassment. There are few things more painful for an editorial writer whose taste has advanced beyond his talent than to go back and read some of his own stuff from years back; maybe that's why I would rather anticipate future editorials than read old ones. But that's unavoidable around this time of year, when the editorial writers' annual convention approaches, and we're all obliged to provide samples of our work for others to examine—all too well.

This week, I've been looking over the editorial pages of three other papers—all respectable, not to say deadly at times—and what they most lack is that Menckenesque sense of serious fun. Either it has been lost in the writing/thinking, or it was never there. When it does burst through, like the sun through heavy mist, the reader is rewarded, enthralled and, like the writer, impelled to think despite himself. But it doesn't happen often enough.

Grover C. Hall Jr. diagnosed this condition in the *Montgomery Advertiser* some thirty years ago when he noted that editors in general seemed "tired and unhappy." Being Grover C. Hall Jr., he couldn't understand it. "What's the matter with 'em anyway?" he wanted to know. "They've got the grandest job in the world." That's something editorial writers should remember when called upon to open a vein. And if that thought doesn't comfort, a writer can be still be forgiven for hating to write—just as long as he doesn't let the writing show it.

Late-Night Thoughts

The Tyranny of the News

Consider this an anti-commentary. The news is too much with us late and soon, and watching and listening we lay waste our powers.

The news seduces and betrays us, mainly by pretending to be new. The names may change but the plots remain remarkably the same, just as weapons may change but war remains the same.

Sometimes even those charged with studying and commenting on the news, like pathologists who bend over petri dishes every day or, in a different time, witches examining entrails, realize that all they want is a day off. There arises a lust for total silence and a merciful end to this insatiable human curiosity that masticates events to death and beyond, and then demands more to mull.

Contrary to Gresham's Law, the bad does not always drive out the good. The new just drives out the old, even when the new is nothing but a revival of the old. See the cycle of trends in fashion, on Broadway, in theology. The question is always the same old one: "What's new?" The phrase has become more greeting than inquiry, so habituated are we to news for entertainment's sake. Nobody asks, "What's old?" And so every variety of the new is paraded before the seeker: the pretend new, the same old new, and the old masquerading as the new. The New Politics. The New Morality. The New Look. The New Republic, which represents the old liberalism. This profusion of the new would be enough to make a reactionary of anybody.

The great advantage of being in love, a German poet once commented, is that one loses all interest in newspapers. Today, he might change that observation only to include television. Try flipping through every channel within 30 seconds in the middle of the night. The result is a whirling kaleidoscope of American life, the West, and the world as seen by some combination of Alfred Hitchcock, Norman Rockwell, Sam Donaldson and Gary Larson. Click: The screen focuses and—

click—dissolves through one Weimaresque scene after another: murder, mayhem, cowboys, car chases, pornography, the ultimate secret of success in business (call our toll-free line), the ultimate secret of success in religion (call our toll-free line), some product in full color one would gladly pay not to have, Ralph Kramden as Jackie Gleason or vice versa, the National Anthem with warplanes, Donna Reed and John Wayne, Freddy Krueger and mutant ninja turtles, an empty static-ridden channel that comes as a blessed relief, car chases, a news analysis in the form of a shouting match, more car chases, the weather as board game, Kirk Douglas, a lion eating a deer again, photogenic people in fashionable clothes saying stupid things at close range....

Click. The silence resounds like salvation. "The desire not to be impinged upon, to be left to oneself, has been a mark of high civilization both on the part of individuals and communities."—Isaiah Berlin. The dark night of the soul, F. Scott Fitzgerald said, comes at 3 o'clock in the morning. Now television makes it even darker in the brightest way.

As art is science in the making, the news is culture in the making. It poses problems. It offers solutions. But in all the channel-flipping, it grows harder to tell the problems from the solutions.

Culture was once the name for the answers. The Spanish philosopher José Ortega y Gasset defined culture as the succession of swimming strokes necessary to survive the shipwreck that is life. But once survival is assured and the strokes no longer necessary, he warned, culture becomes a useless ritual. And "this culture, on being received by later generations, becomes more complicated and loses more and more of its genuineness. It turns into affectation and a concern with the topical, into cultural narcissism and the dead letter. Man then loses himself again, becomes demoralized, not now in the primitive forest, but in the excessive vegetation of his own culture." Can Sr. Ortega have watched much television? Or were the newspapers of his day sufficient to grant him this ever more relevant insight?

Not to worry. There is always something to break through the news-induced coma and bring back untelevised reality—as sharply, as unmistakably as stubbing your toe in the dark. Sometimes the news shatters its own spell and reveals what is really out there. "LONDON (AP)—A senior Iranian cleric today offered up to $2.6 million for the slaying of Salman Rushdie, whose novel *The Satanic Verses* has angered Moslem fundamentalists. Newspapers said the writer was under armed guard."

All the Cambridge-educated author did was write another best-seller with some teasing references to the sacred that he denied were teasing references to the sacred. Have we become so inured to sacrilege that we can no longer recognize it when we see or, or even when we write it? Like any other mod author, Salman Rushdie just borrowed a name here and there from the appropriate scripture, and found he had aroused a non-Cambridge, non-Western, non-kaleidoscopic world that was no longer supposed to exist. And it was offering millions for his head. Good morning, Mr. Rushdie, this is your wake-up call.

One cannot approve of this. One is well bred. One believes in freedom of the press, in tolerating the usual level of sacrilege in mod society. One believes in the West, for that matter, and that it still exists at 3 o'clock in the morning somewhere beyond television, beyond the never-ending news, beyond the endless products being bought and sold, sold, sold. Why, then, is there something perversely satisfying in this one piece of news? Because it reminds that there is still a sharp, teeming real world out there that cannot be captured, boiled down and served up whole on the endless tape that is the news.

Suddenly we are reminded of how fragile our imitation of reality is, how fluid its phantasmagoric foundations. Beyond the thin shell that is the West, seeping underneath it, there remains the sea incarnadine still roiled by inquisition, pogrom, and *hashshashin*, the Arabic root of our word Assassin. And its waves can be felt.

Furore still reigns and will not be put off by explanations about how this has all been a misunderstanding. (Salman Rushdie, as quoted by Reuters: "The thing that is most disturbing is that they are talking about a book that doesn't exist. The book that is worth killing people for and burning flags for is not the book that I wrote.") Nothing puzzles modern man more than being taken seriously.

Early this century, when the Media monster was still in its infancy, the disaster of the day was the sinking of an ocean liner that the great god News had said was unsinkable. The world was saddened, yet here and there a few isolated souls were strangely assured. "The sinking of the Titanic," Alexander Blok confided to a friend, "has made me indescribably happy; there is, despite everything, an ocean."

IV | THE SMALL TOWN

Entirely Personal

This essay is based on Paul Greenberg's acceptance speech on receiving the William Allen White Award at the University of Kansas on February 10, 1988.

To the many who have come to admire and hope to emulate him, his full name was not William Allen White.

His full name was William Allen White from Emporia.

And he most of all knew it.

His first editorial for the *Emporia Gazette*, on June 3rd, 1895, was headed "Entirely Personal," and it began this way:

"To the gentle reader who may, through the coming years during which we are spared to one another, follow the course of this paper, a word of personal address from the new editor of the Gazette is due.

"In the first place, the new editor hopes to live here until he is the old editor, until some of the visions which rise before him as dreams shall have come true.

"He hopes always to sign 'from Emporia' after his name when he is abroad, and he trusts that he may so endear himself to the people that they will be as proud of the first words of the signature as he is of the last....

"He expects to perform all the kind offices of the country editor in this community for a generation to come. It is likely that he will write

89

the wedding notices of the boys and girls in the schools; that he will announce the birth of the children who will some day honor Emporia, and that he will say the final words over those of middle age who read these lines.

"His relations with the people of this town and county are to be close and personal...."

How different that is from the Blanding of American Journalism that has occurred since William Allen White defined his place in the world with those simple and still affecting lines. Who knows where today's anchorpersons are from, and what difference would it make if we did? Their value would seem to reside not in any close, personal relation with a particular place but precisely in their depersonalization. The lack of a specific locale now becomes a warrant of objectivity and expertise; it certifies an ability to communicate with all—since it is clear that we no longer communicate with anyone in particular.

It takes only a momentary glance to see what the market calls for in Mass Communicators, who now have replaced journalists just as journalists replaced newspapermen. The demand is for the pseudo-personal, a style designed—fabricated, you might say—to reflect a personal flavor but never risk offending. The result is a nationally uniform voice that dares not betray any distinctive accent, strong belief, or particular geographical origin—lest it exclude a single reader or viewer. It is a style that is to personality as NutraSweet is to sugar.

An increasingly impersonal society, in which the closest approach to intimacy and conviction is the devout wish that we all Have a Nice Day, demands a simulacrum of the personal. The market calls for Ken and Barbie lookalikes with personalities as blown-dry as their hair. It is not ideas or insights that mark the mod communicator, but a blend of careful coiffure and a sincerely antiseptic manner that goes by the misnomer Style and would better be described as the lack of it. The political column is now said to be a dying art, and Personal Journalism is something that was practiced in the 19th Century—as though any journalism that ever affected us was not personal.

Westbrook Pegler would surely be advised today to go into some other line of work. Murray Kempton, my own nominee for the best columnist writing today, is so well admired—by the too few who can read him regularly—because he is an anachronism: a stylist whose roots in the gentilities of old Baltimore are as clear as his devotion to staying a local writer in New York. In such a voice there is a sense of place, with that place's distinctive words and ways and code.

Perhaps the saddest aspect of today's journalism is that a sense of place is not missed, at least not consciously. We have only a vague feeling that something is no longer there. And so we go on to the next vacuous offering, and the next, in an unsuccessful search for what we don't exactly know, much like the late-night viewer twiddling the dial of his television set, already more asleep than awake.

There once were writers who knew where they were from, and so were able to tell the rest of us where we were going. Like William Allen White from Emporia. I blame William Allen White for destroying one of my favorite definitions of journalism—"Journalism is writing that will be less interesting tomorrow." I have read some of his editorials written almost a century ago. They not only interest. They move.

I cherish an old photograph of the passengers aboard the S.S. *Argentina*, taken when it arrived with a shipload of immigrants at the Port of Boston on February 10th, 1921—67 years ago today. If you look carefully, and if you know what you're looking for, you'll find the face of a 19-year-old girl—broad, Slavic features, pug nose, fair skin, dark hair drawn severely back, unsmiling in the photographic style of those days. A face indistinguishable from millions of others—from the tens of millions of others from Eastern Europe who flocked to the Golden Land between the 1880s and 1920s.

That is the face of my mother, Sarah the daughter of Paesach the miller in the village of Mordt in eastern Poland. Actually, she was from outside the village of Mordt, a country girl traveling alone to the New World with not much more than the clothes on her back and an address clutched in her hand. But if you look closely, you can see in her eyes the hidden treasure she had brought with her through the chaos of what in our innocence was then called The Great War, as if there would not soon be a greater one. Those eyes are full of determination, the determination above all to belong somewhere at last. You can still see that same look, and that same determination, at airports and dockside and citizenship ceremonies—on the faces of new arrivals from Latin America, Southeast Asia, and around the world. America is still America to them. I am grateful for, and very much aware of the honor paid me today; it bears a great and cherished name, a name I long have admired. But I must tell you that, long before today, February 10th has been a great day in my family.

In an age in which the entire globe can be compressed into one photograph from outer space, we tend to forget the power and importance of the single human face, and the longing for roots, a longing that modernity not only conspires to obscure but assures us is no longer important. William Allen White—William Allen White *from Emporia*—knew better. He spoke with such authority on a variety of themes because he knew where he was from, and what he was committed to. Of course he had an unfair advantage. He had Emporia; he had Kansas. When he wrote to friends and neighbors, he did not have to imagine them. They weren't a composite reader survey or a Nielsen rating. They were not some vague, amorphous mass. That helps explain why his prose wasn't amorphous, either. His neighbors' ways were his, their distinctiveness and honor his own. He was part of . . . a community, and he wrote like it, even and especially when he was standing up to it.

In a town like Emporia or Pine Bluff, in a place that is still of a human scale, things are closer to the surface. There is not as much distance between the outward and inward. Make no mistake: It is no swift or easy thing to know a place. As Jacob discovers in Scripture, it may be necessary to leave and return to know a place for the first time. It requires time even to suspect the dimensions of what one does not know. One can no more know a small town at a glance than one can a great city. A Winesburg, Ohio, is as intricate and touching and human and various as any great metropolis, as Sherwood Anderson demonstrated. But there is an advantage in choosing a small community to understand. There are fewer distractions, less insulation.

Life is short everywhere, but it is harder to forget that in a small town. Contrary to the common, unexamined assumption, there is less room for parochial judgments in a small town. There aren't enough people in a small community for each of us to go through life associating only with our own class or persuasion or kind. We have to get to know one another, with all our obvious warts and unexpected virtues, personal crotchets and curious graces. The poor can't be shuffled out of sight quite as neatly. It isn't as easy to hide from responsibility, which may explain the abundance of volunteers in small-town America.

Remember John Winthrop's old vision? "To be a city on the hill," he told his fellow Puritans, "we must bear one another's burdens. We must look not only to our own things, but on the things of our brethren. We must rejoice together, mourn together, labor and suffer together." There is an old American concept that isn't much heard of these days: commonweal. William Allen White understood it. The Emporias of America teach it as nothing else can.

It was once said of another editor of the *Pine Bluff Commercial*, Walter B. Sorrells Jr., "He was successful because he won the respect and the regard of everyone who knew him in a small community, and that's doing it the hard way because in a small community, one cannot hide his deficiencies by remoteness. There is nothing as shrewdly and knowingly and justly critical in its judgments as a small community. A phoney cannot pass for the real thing. One's fellows know him for what he is." Don't choose a small town if you want to hide. In the end, old Jonah found Nineveh a soft touch but he never had to take on an Emporia, or a Pine Bluff.

A lot of small towns are disappearing or, just as fatal, changing from county seat to suburb of some all-encroaching megalopolis. More important are the ways in which we are not changing. The Emporias and Pine Bluffs represent not just a Standard Metropolitan Statistical Area but a way of life, and not just a way of life but a code. That code isn't always observed—but it is always there. Thorstein Veblen, who could not be accused of being a romantic, once observed that "the country town is one of the great American institutions; perhaps the greatest, in the sense that it has had....a greater part than any other in shaping public sentiment and giving character to American culture."

William Allen White, country editor, understood as much, in large part because he proposed to shape public sentiment and give character to American culture. And he did. He does even unto this day. He lay down each night, the battle waged, and rose up afresh each morning to fight the good fight and, most important, to have a good time doing it. What more could a newspaperman ask? Of course he was aware of journalism's sins—those of commission and, far worse, of omission—but he wasted no time agonizing or repining. He had words to write and wrongs to correct and a place to tie to. He lived and felt and thought, and there are few occupations better suited for those activities than that of country editor. Mr. White knew something too many of us forget: why we got into this business in the first place. This job is fun. Is there anything more enjoyable than a prize seat at the human comedy, or anything more conducive to growth than the realization that we are part of the show?

To quote from a speech Eugene Patterson of the *St. Petersburg Times* gave on this campus—". . . . always one knew, reading William Allen White, that he was a true believer in his free democracy, and no mere scold of its imperfections. Perhaps we take more for granted than he did, and need to revive our sense of the majesty of this free nation even as we expose its failings and flaws. I believe he might tell us to write from our hearts as well as our spleens. Above all, I am sure he would remind us editors of our first obligation: to cover and serve the particular communities where we live, and make our livings. He knew the policemen and the shopkeepers and the schoolteachers of Emporia by name, and while he might argue with them and alienate some by his headstrong impressions of what was best for the community, they knew he (cared) about the community, and thought of its best interest with a mind undiverted by lesser concerns or scattered holdings."

I would add only that Editor White was not only headstrong but heart strong, and I wish his tribe would increase. This award leaves a country editor proud, and a little uneasy in the shade of a great name, and eager to get back home and produce some deserving editorials. It is a fine occasion and, conscious of it, I would like to share something fine. It is a brief admonition I had to learn long before I could understand it; it is a chapter from *Pirke Avot*, the treatise of the Talmud dealing with ethical matters. Originally intended for rabbis and other interpreters of the law, it says more in less time about the ethics of my trade than I've ever been able to glean from any number of lectures and seminars. It consists of three injunctions:

—Love creative work.

—Do not seek dominance over others.

—And avoid intimacy with the ruling powers.

I have no way of knowing how much trouble this concise guide to the ethics of journalism has kept me out of; I do know that every time I've forgotten it, I wished I hadn't.

The Talmud also says something that helps explain the extraordinary influence of a country editor from Emporia, Kansas. Recognition, it says, flees from those who pursue it, and pursues those who flee from it.

The *Emporia Gazette* never had more than 7,000 subscribers when William Allen White was its editor, yet he was able to stir a nation. Maybe that was because readers could never be quite sure what he would say next. He had an American affinity for the unpredictable, and an American contempt for any party line. H. L. Mencken, no stickler for conformity or consistency himself, would say of him: "Of all the American Liberals, Bill White of Emporia is the most persnickety, perverse, pernicious, and periodic. He is the most often mistaken, inconstant, inconsistent, unwise, short-sighted, percipient, emotional, banal, self-righteous, self-critical, partisan and independent, generally maddening and altogether loveable conservative in the country."

What a grand model for an American opinionator. He was that rarest of American political fauna today, a Republican who thinks. William Allen White was also that most common of American species—the small-town boy who, no matter how far he goes or how sophisticated he becomes, cannot shake his sense of decency, or his delight with the world.

Editor White understood that his best friends and severest critics were the same people—his neighbors and his readers, and that his best work was a direct response to his town. He wrote his famous editorial—"What's the Matter With Kansas?"—in angry response after being besieged by a gang of Populists a block from his office. When it appeared, Mrs. White was afraid that this time her husband had gone too far. So was Mr. White, who confided in his autobiography, "Well, there is another of those foolish impulsive things that I do which seem all right at the time but which I know when it is too late are inspired in a habitual unwisdom in me that amounts to a major weakness."

As he soon discovered, and as we all know now, William Allen White wrote that editorial from strength, not weakness. He didn't have a morning editorial conference to talk him out of it; he had to go with his best instincts, as many a small-town editor still must. He was able to write his best and, yes, his worst, and learn from both—a luxury only small newspapers seem able to afford their editors. When I was one of five editorial writers at the late *Chicago Daily News*, I once proposed that, instead of all five of us coming in every day, each one of us work just one day a week. The rest would stay home instead of talking away each other's best and most personal ideas every morning. The rest of the editorial board clearly thought that was another of my perverse jokes. Now the *Chicago Daily News* has no need of even a single editorial writer. And the *Emporia Gazette* goes on.

Somebody ought to write an editorial that could be headed, "What's the Matter With Editors?" Someone already has. Back in the 1950s, our occupational disease was already evident to Grover C. Hall Jr. of the *Montgomery Advertiser*. His diagnosis still holds up. Here is how it begins:

> "We who hate your gaudy guts salute you."
> So wrote the Republican editor, William Allen White, in *The Emporia Gazette* when Roosevelt won his dazzling victory in 1936 over Landon.
> It is our estimate that there are not today a dozen editors practicing in this country on major newspapers who would have said it that way even had they thought of it. Such salty, indecorous, vivid speech is something from which today's editorial pages recoil.
> Not a dozen editors would use that robust language and

would sack an associate if he did it on his own, yet they will agree that White was the foremost editor of his era.

Something is wrong here. We say it's today's editorial writers. They have the most powerful speaking platform in the world and while their influence is plainly great, it is by no means as great as it would be if the editorials were written by men of much talent and few inhibitions.

Grover Hall Jr. ended that editorial with some words that are more relevant than ever:

> Last year one of the topflight editors remarked to us that, in general, editors were "tired and unhappy." Our conviction on that isn't matured yet, but looking about at the last two sessions of the American Society of Newspaper Editors and one of the National Conference of Editorial Writers we found ourselves nearing agreement. What's the matter with 'em anyway?—they've got the grandest job in the world.

William Allen White understood that his was a grand job; he made it grand, with a little invaluable help from a small town. He was shaped by Emporia as surely as Galena molded Sam Grant and Independence produced Harry Truman. William Allen White was cussed and discussed by a town that was many things but above all, and below it all, it was a town rooted in its time and place. Emporia, like the rest of Kansas, has standards—in great part because William Allen White helped shape them. My old publisher at the *Pine Bluff Commercial*, E.W. Freeman III, used to tell me that a newspaper had to share the standards of its community in order to communicate effectively, and at the same time raise them. That's a neat trick, but it may be about the only one worth doing with an editorial page. William Allen White pulled it off in his time, and it's an assignment that still wants doing.

A word to those journalism students who will soon be looking for a place to work and, incidentally, to live. Allow me to suggest that in your search you consider the qualities that drew William Allen White to Emporia, and helped make him William Allen White. Such a place offers a point of vantage that the trendiest part of this business cannot match—does not wish to match. You can see a ways on the plains of Kansas, and see simple things.

By all means, if what you've wanted all your life is to get away from Kansas and small towns, go. You've got a good education and a green light. We'll follow your progress, be proud of you, and, most important, we'll wait for you. And if it should occur to you down the road that maybe you've left something behind, something of importance and duration, something to tie to, remember that the Emporias and Pine Bluffs are still here. Don't keep us waiting too long. There are things to be said, words that need writing. And there is no substitute for time in coming to know your place, your people, yourself.

I regret to inform any of you who want to write the Great American Novel that it's already been done, perhaps more than once. F. Scott Fitzgerald's *The Great Gatsby* would surely be in the running for that distinction. There is an observation on its last page that might provide an appropriate note on which to end these remarks. It goes like this:

"I thought of Gatsby's wonder when he first picked out the green light at the end of Daisy's dock. He had come a long way to this blue lawn, and his dream must have seemed so close that he could hardly fail to grasp it. He did not know that it was already behind him, somewhere back in that vast obscurity behind the city, where the dark fields of the republic rolled on under the night."

Why I Live Here

This essay is adapted from a talk to the national convention of Associated Press Managing Editors in Cincinnati, which included a discussion on "Why Journalists Choose to Stay in Small Towns."

"Why do you stay in Pine Bluff?"

I can't count the number of times I've heard that question addressed to local businessmen, ministers, teachers—not to mention the handyman and friend who comes out to our house whenever we have a problem with the air conditioning. His answer is to sort of shrug his shoulders, allow as how it's as good a town as any, and mention that his old assistant is just back from a few years in Houston, having enjoyed the big city about as much as he could stand.

The notion that people pick the towns where they live on the basis of some impersonal statistical tabulation is perpetuated by publications like Rand McNally's *Places Rated Almanac.* Everything I know about people says it ain't necessarily so.

Rand McNally has nine statistical standards for a place to live, which it presents with great certitude and no feeling. Its nine criteria do matter: climate and terrain, housing, health care and environment, crime, transportation, education, recreation, the arts, and economics. But none of them matter much in isolation from the more personal aspects of a town, such as my own nine:

1. The spiritual quality of a community.

2. The town's Courtesy Level, which may be defined as the sum of civilities a total stranger could reasonably expect to encounter there.

3. Rootedness—a quality closely related to sense of place.

4. Diversity.

5. Loyalty, which is not to be confused with conformity. This loyalty is not only to one's neighbors but to one's principles. One of the qualities that makes Pine Bluff so attractive is the room it leaves for individuality, for what one resident called Creative Disagreement.

6. Generosity, including a generosity of spirit.

7. Pride, also known as self-respect, and not to be confused with simple boosterism or public relations.

8. Tolerance.

9. Openness.

How judge a place without consulting standards like these other nine? Any town could measure up in all of Rand McNally's categories and, without these other qualities, be hard to distinguish from Hell.

Whether a place turns out to have such qualities will be up to the individual in a small town in a way it can't be to one of the countless myriads in a great city. There is no hiding in a small town, and not much chance of escaping into anonymity. The newspaperman who writes about folks is going to see them the next day, and have to live with them. When he messes up, it's an embarrassment that can't be hidden. When he triumphs, his community does.

It's good for the character, this awareness of being watched. A Talmudic sage once theorized that men fear other men more than they do God, since they would do things in God's presence that they would never think of committing before the eyes of their fellow man. It's not as easy to escape those eyes in a small town, or to escape the responsibility of having to take a stand from time to time.

Yes, by Rand McNally's not very deep standards, choosing to live in a small town may demand certain sacrifices. But if the standard of living isn't as high, that doesn't mean the standard of life is any lower. On the contrary, people in small towns *have* to be more involved. There aren't that many of us; it isn't as easy to hide from responsibility and live an isolated life among your own class, religion, race or political persuasion. Maybe that explains the persistence of volunteers in small-town America; there isn't anybody else to do the job around here if we won't.

There is something offensive about the underlying assumption of tabulations like Rand McNally's, namely that people will choose a place to live on the basis of what they can get out of it. There is something in us all that seeks not just what we can get but what we can give. There is a chance to know and shape a small town—in a way it would never be possible to know and shape a great city. A small town is a constant refutation of the impersonal and statistical, a place where people will constantly surprise you. That is, if you're still open to surprise, and not lost in the kind of sophistication that big cities and big newspapers may inspire.

Yes, there are things you have to put up with in a smaller community. Perhaps the most irritating is the inferiority complex that prompts the common question, "Why do you stay in Pine Bluff?" As though staying had to be explained, not leaving. Leaving may make sense by Rand McNally's standards but not by real ones. The same inferiority complex prompts that strange question one invariably hears at an elegant party, or even at the opening of a new shopping mall in town: "Can you believe this is Pine Bluff?"

What's not to believe? It's not the predictable extension of uniform national culture that is incredible: it's that we're holding on to as much of our past, of our eccentricities, of *ourselves* as we do. That's the remarkable accomplishment in an increasingly homogenized culture. As a small-town boy from Hannibal, Missouri, commented after he had become Mark Twain, world-famous author, and was touring India: "All the *me* in me is in a little Missouri village halfway around the world." Why do so many Americans listen religiously to Garrison Keillor every Saturday night to hear the news from Lake Wobegon? Is it just nostalgia? I suspect it's a hankering for something more, something that may be present everywhere but is closer to the surface in a small town. It's human feeling, and naturally it's more evident in a community that is still on a human scale.

It would be a pleasure to talk shop a little longer with friends old and new at an interesting convention in a grand old city. But, you see, tonight is All-Civic Night in Pine Bluff, when we recognize those volunteers whose year-long efforts give our town something of its own distinctive flavor. And I wouldn't want to miss it. I want to see who gets singled out, and honor all those volunteers, and see my friends, neighbors, and critics—who often enough turn out to be one and the same. I'm sure you understand, especially if you come from a small town.

A Small Town of the Mind

The ideal small town, as anyone who grew up in one will attest, has some definite and palpable characteristics, immediately recognizable to the cognoscenti. Like neon lights. And a single main street, preferably called Main Street. And a multitude of small shops, and a sense of an immense amount of local lore waiting just beneath the simplest surface. It should not only be small but, more important, seem so.

Was it an ancient Greek who theorized that democratic government was possible only in a city-state small enough for each citizen to recognize every other? The population therefore shouldn't be more than 5,000 or so, or at least it shouldn't feel like much more than 5,000. Every storefront on Main Street should be occupied, and there must be a water tower on which the name of the town is proudly emblazoned in three-foot-high letters.

There should be a memorable sign or two, like the Sunbeam girl at the foot of Main Street in Pine Bluff, or the huge bespectacled eyes of Doctor T. J. Eckleburg, optometrist, in *The Great Gatsby*. The local department store need not actually have pneumatic tubes to deliver change to the customers, but it should have one of those displays of garments—say three or four little girl's dresses—all pinned to a large swath of cloth and prominently displayed in a front window. Or maybe a dozen child's sweaters on little hangers.

And every small town needs a keystone, a social institution that holds the rest of the place together. Not a city hall or a county courthouse, although those will do in a pinch, but a fire station or, even better, a coffee shop where the sun pours in through generous windows on bright mornings, a place to have doughnuts in the morning and a forum for businessmen in the middle of the afternoon. It should come complete with blue plate specials and waitresses everybody knows—a place Where The Elite Meet to Eat, crowded at mealtimes but permeated with a bright Edward Hopper loneliness in the middle of a Sunday afternoon. It must have a long black-and-white tile counter with a neat row of stools alongside, separated by a wide aisle from the serious eaters seated at the tables or tucked into the booths. Ideally, the windows would give a full view of Main Street to anyone in the place. This perfect small town of the mind would have a small park across the street where a great old live oak towers above a few inviting benches.

Can such a place still exist? One recalls a dirty trick George Orwell once played. He wrote a most serious recommendation for an idyllic English pub—spacious, quiet but convivial, where the children could wander in and out, or play in the adjoining garden while their parents socialized over a pint and where the warm beer was served in china mugs—never cold, inhuman glasses. But at the end of his description, the author had to admit that no such place still existed in his time.

I am happy to report that this coffee shop, and town, does—unless I was hallucinating one Sunday awhile back. The water tower that one can spy from the booths in the coffee shop is plainly marked LUCEDALE. It's right on Highway 98 between Hattiesburg and Mobile in deepest Mississippi. This coffee shop, restaurant, social center, and three-dimensional Edward Hopper painting is called The Coffee Pot. (Member, Miss. Restaurant Assn., opened 1937 by Raymond and Evelyn Bailey.) The place is advertised by an unmistakable neon replica of a coffee pot eternally pouring. Each of the seven big plate-glass windows fronts directly on Main Street, so one can see and be seen. Each has some latticework at the top from which is suspended a large wooden replica of a coffee pot. The ceiling fans turn as inexorably as time.

The menu is heavy on grits and chicken—half a chicken with french fries, green salad and hot rolls went for $3.25, the oyster loaf for $2.95. But sophistication has made inroads. The special of the day was quiche lorraine. Or as the menu obligingly listed it, "quiche lorraine (Keesh)." No cover charge, no airs.

It's the kind of place two local matrons might leave arm in arm after Sunday dinner while their husbands brought up the rear. One almost expects the coffee cups to bear the once mandatory green stripe around the rim and the suits advertised across the street to come with two pairs of pants. From the booth, one can see Fail's Burial Insurance across the street—affording the visitor both a piquant name and a *memento mori*. Time may have passed Lucedale by, but I couldn't. Not after I saw that neon coffee pot in the air like a vision. It's the way small towns are supposed to look, and still do in the storybooks. There's even an unlikely landmark: A scratching post, which is a kind of street sign with notches for scratching your back.

Small towns, like spinach and Scotch, may be an acquired taste. Whether you like them may depend on where you've grown up. When the Russian poet Yevgeny Yevtushenko visited this country, he was asked which part of America he liked best, and he immediately replied: Alaska. Turns out he was from Siberia. For people who carry small towns around in their minds and memories, Lucedale, Miss., is not to be missed. You can always tell a town by its coffee shop. And as long as Pine Bluff has places like John Noah's, the Country Kitchen and The 1020, there's hope for us, too.

America: She's Still Out Here

One of the sadder and more relevant comments on the State of the Union comes, as it often does, from a foreign observer. Manzoor Ahmad, chairman of the department of philosophy at the University of Karachi, is spending some time as a visiting professor at the University of the South. When the *Sewanee News* asked him for his chief criticism of American society, he said this:

"Everything good over here becomes an industry. Even emotion becomes an industry. Man-to-man, person-to-person relationships are mediated through institutions. I see ads on TV asking, do you want to adopt a foster child, then send money to such and such a foundation. Don't you think that may be why so many people want dogs? The social distances between people grow each day as a result of the way your cities are built and your society is organized. Your emotions are becoming impersonal."

And also unrealistic, impractical, artificial, precious, self-absorbed, and inflexible. That's what happens when human emotions are engaged safely apart from actual humans. This is the flip side of the tendency that de Tocqueville praised as "associational activities" in his classic *Democracy in America*—meaning the American impulse to turn every good work into an organized effort. We are a nation of joiners. On a small scale back in the 1830s, such cooperation was the salvation and creation of frontier society. On the huge, industrialized, televised scale of the 1980s, the human factor is eliminated. What remains is the tendency to be linked together in ever larger and less personal organizations. The result is an atomized society.

If there is one dominant theme of so much late-night television, it is loneliness—and the various ways to escape it that only make it even more desperate. The distinction between a healing solitude and a desperate loneliness has never been one that Americans had a talent for understanding, and television has only aggravated that failing.

One suspects that Dr. Ahmad got his impression of America not so much from the small town of Sewanee, Tenn., as from the endless, borderless realm of late-night television. That is where one finds the commercials for foster children and 101 other vicarious forms of moral gratification. All come pre-packaged with electronic images— why take a messy, unpredictable risk like human contact?

Strangely enough, it is television or some equally McLuhanesque medium that has come to give things their sense of reality in this country—the way snapshots of the grandchildren once did. Pictures tend to be so much more graphic/adorable/convenient than mere reality. If there is any institution in society that validates our existence, it is not government or art or religion or even business—which was the ultimate gauge of reality in Calvin Coolidge's America. Now the ultimate validator of American existence is the omnipresent telescreen.

Andy Warhol said something about everybody being guaranteed 15 minutes of fame, which reduces fame to a fleeting notoriety. Fame may no longer even be possible in a society that has substituted celebrity for it; our attention span may not be long enough. "Fame is the one that does not stay," wrote Emily Dickinson, anticipating and admonishing modernity. But how could she have seen that the ultimate judge of such things would be encased in a little box no broader than its vision?

A deputy minister in Canada said it a few years ago: "We have virtually reached the point where no idea, policy or event can enjoy more than the most shadowy existence unless it has been consecrated by the media of mass communications." And *consecrated* is just the right verb. If the ancient Greeks held that the unexamined life is not worth living, today it is the untelevised one. And who could sympathize more readily with today's craving for identity than a deputy minister in Canada? I forget his name.

Amidst all the electronic sound and fury that passes for signifying, it was a comfort and assurance to see a school of journalism and mass communications honor Charles Kuralt, this year's recipient of the William Allen White award from the University of Kansas. For more than two decades, he has covered America while the Big Boys were busy describing an unreasonable facsimile.

"We all have our duties at CBS News," Mr. Kuralt explained. "Dan Rather and Mike Wallace and those guys have theirs, and I have mine. Mine is to be sure that no musical saw player, or swimming pig, or fellow who has a car that runs on corncobs goes unremarked on national television. My standing instructions are: If I come upon a real news story out there On The Road, to be sure to call some real reporter to cover it." And to make unreal news of it.

It's hard to escape the suspicion that the reality of America is being lost, or has never been found, by the tellers of The Big Story. Quoting Charles Kuralt is an irresistible temptation because his talk at the University of Kansas articulated what so many of us have felt about this trade, namely:

"Journalism talks loudly, and speeds along. The country talks softly and goes slowly. Even if the great question in Washington is how many billions it will take to bail out the savings and loans, out in the country, the kids still have to be got off to school on time. I am persuaded that journalism would be better off if it could find ways of attuning itself more closely to the rhythm and worries and joys of the country. Listening is a virtue of journalism that is easily overlooked in a time when we journalists so much enjoy hearing ourselves talk."

William Allen White said it: A great editorial is one that says something everybody knows but nobody has said before. Charles Kuralt's talk at Lawrence, Kan., was a great editorial. It's good to have him on the road, and good to know that the road is still there, full of Americans who may never be validated by television but validate their own lives every day.

There may be a reason why a movie like *It's a Wonderful Life,* no great hit in its own time, has struck a chord with a new generation of Americans. One suspects that its small-town hero, George Bailey of Bailey Building and Loan, would be much sounder on the subject of how to restore the country's savings-and-loans than the hotshots who got them into trouble—or the equally assured Washington experts who, having watched this mess develop, are now going to clean it up.

There is a strange kind of despair that haunts a society like ours, adrift in peace and prosperity. Charles Kuralt's coverage of a different, broader, more basic America is a useful antidote. In reviewing the greatest, most enduring, most liberating changes he has witnessed in his decades at this trade, Mr. Kuralt commented: "None of these changes originated under the dome of the Capitol or in the big white house on Pennsylvania Avenue. (They) all were born out there in the country, which is how democracy is supposed to work, as I understand it."

Mr. Kuralt's big story has yet to lead the 5 o'clock news or make Page One. It's the same story de Tocqueville reported in another century, and it's still happening. Here's the way Charles Kuralt reported it from Kansas: "...on the road, visiting and revisiting every part of every state many times, I haven't been able to keep from noticing that something is going on you don't hear much about or read much about. It is this: That there are many Americans quietly concerning themselves with purposes and undertakings here at home that are decent, and compassionate, and unsullied by arrogance, or hostility to others, or delusions of superiority, or motives of greed...a kind of conspiracy of good people who don't even know one another, but each of whom has come to see the grace and worth and joy of acting themselves to solve problems and heal wounds and help their neighbors...people who care about their communities as much as they care about themselves."

Maybe that's because in towns the size of Lawrence, Kan., or Pine Bluff, Ark., it's a little easier to see that our communities *are* ourselves. Validation doesn't have to come from without when it comes from within.

Dr. Ahmad from Karachi, meet Mr. Kuralt from CBS. Meet America. You'll like her.

It's a Wonderful Life

To many Americans, this season would not be complete without at least a few scenes from *It's a Wonderful Life*. The movie wasn't much of a hit when it was first released just after the Second World War, but it has slowly acquired an immense popularity—and even a certain critical acclaim. Perhaps that is because it represents a peculiarly American vision. It is not a vision of Christmas—despite that last, tear-wrenching scene in front of the tree—but of a society, and how it ought to be.

This year I read a brief analysis of the movie by a professor of American Studies at Boston University, and it got me thinking not so much about the movie as about the consistent misunderstandings of professors. Professor Ray Carney has written a book about Frank Capra's films entitled *American Vision*. He says the movie shows that, while life can be "an enriching Norman Rockwell experience, it also can be smothering, where you end up marrying the girl you went to high school with, and you never get to go to Europe.... It tells us George is one of the most sad and lonely and tragic characters ever imagined. I cry when I see it."

I confess to having shed a few tears over "It's a Wonderful Life" myself—but not for the professor's reasons. Nothing in the movie seems as sad as the professor's analysis of it. George Bailey a tragic figure? Why, he's the richest man in town, as his brother says at the end of the movie. He makes Mr. Potter, that old miser, look like a pauper—because George Bailey has loved and sacrificed and built and given and stood alone a time or two, and, well, he has lived. He has not gone through life as a tourist.

Not getting to Europe does not strike me as the kind of experience that qualifies for tragedy, possibly because I know some Americans who were born there. To them, not coming to America would have been the tragedy. Surely only an American would be so bereft of the tragic sense of life as to consider marrying your high school sweetheart a tragedy. These latitudes are simply not hospitable to the tragic art, though in the go-getting American spirit, we can compete with the best of foreigners in that department. See *The Great Gatsby*. But "It's a Wonderful Life" is not an entry in the tragedy department.

The movie's message is that George Bailey has not led a sad, lonely or tragic life, much as he might think so in his more self-pitying moments. (Can the professor, like so many Americans, be using "tragic" as a synonym for sad? It is a common American misusage, and says much about the nature of our history. Lacking common experience with the real thing, we call everything from a fender-bender to a bankruptcy a tragedy.)

On these shores, tragedy in its original, legitimate Greek sense flourishes only with care and feeding, while in Europe, where the concept originated, it seems to come naturally. Perhaps it is the American insistence on happy endings, onstage and off, that makes our definition of tragedy decidedly less than Aristotelian.

If there is a moral to Frank Capra's movie, it may be the comment from Clarence, George's bumbling guardian angel: "Strange, isn't it? Each man's life touches so many other lives, and when he isn't around he leaves an awful hole to fill, doesn't he? . . . You see, George, you really had a wonderful life. Don't you see what a mistake it would be to throw it away?" That's a lot more Eugene Field than Aristotle.

The movie is a celebration of the usual American virtues, which have never been usual enough. To quote Nancy Dillon, a writer who can remember watching the film with her father: "We laughed, and cried, a lot that afternoon, and at the end I no longer saw my father as being at all ordinary." There are few things more extraordinary than the ordinary virtues of small-town, middle-class America.

Nancy Dillon, it might be noted, lives in Worthington, Ohio—which sounds not unlike the movie's Bedford Falls. The values of Bedford Falls are those our professional intellectuals are supposed to see through. Sometimes they are so busy seeing through them that they don't see them at all. Or they confuse the happy with the sad, the lonely with the interconnected, and, strangest of all, the triumphant with the tragic. Just as George Bailey did for a while.

Equally undiscerning are those who would idealize small towns; they don't see the potential Pottersville inside every Bedford Falls. Just one man, like George Bailey, can make the difference. Think of all those who make a difference in your town—and of all those who don't.

The most unsettling aspect of the popularity now accorded *It's a Wonderful Life* is the realization that nostalgia for certain values tends to set in just when they are disappearing. Happily, nostalgia can bring them back, for there are fashions in values just as there are in clothes.

Jimmy Stewart, the actor who is George Bailey's alter ego, was once asked to explain the movie's popularity, and he responded: "In spite of all the things that have happened and the things that seem to be going wrong, I think it shows that George Bailey's values are still prevalent in this country and are in no danger of being knocked down." That does not sound like a tragic character talking. It sounds like George Bailey after Clarence has straightened him out. The distinguished professor's view of George as a tragic figure strikes me as sadder than anything in the movie, but at least it's not tragic. It's more comic, this being America. I wish the professor a merry Christmas, a happy New Year, and a wonderful life.

Manners and Morals

What is the best mannered city in the country?

No one who has ever had the privilege of visiting Charleston, S.C., will be surprised to find that an unscientific but highly credible poll of business executives has awarded the palm to Charleston—for the second time.

Manners are another outward sign of an inward grace, and those looking for the secret of Charleston's success would do well to admire her soul as well. Just as behind all those well-preserved homes there is pride, so behind Charleston's smiles and warmth there is a genuine regard for others that many of us have felt. Which do you think came first—the outward form or the inward substance? It's as simple a question as the one about the chicken and the egg. Each leads to the other.

It is a sign of the times, and a judgment on them, that there is now more than enough emphasis on urbanization, capitalization and manipulation (always called image-building) but precious little on manners. The very word has acquired a quaint, superficial, even optional sound. The notion that good manners are the essence of society might bemuse, or even amuse, the modern go-getter. He would have to be convinced that manners pay some dividend before assigning them a place on his Must-Do list for today.

The notion that the essence of manners is that they are for others, that they are not means but end, sounds alien in mod America, not least in some of its manners courses—the kind that put form before essence. There is a difference between the two. In *To Kill a Mockingbird*, Atticus Finch pours molasses over his bread—so that a visiting play-mate of his daughter's who pours molasses over everything will feel at home. That is the essence of manners though it violates the form.

Yes, there is something unseemly, almost unmannerly, in listing cities by the quality of their manners. It is to reduce a very noticeable but not very measurable quality to another statistic. But if this list rekindles some interest in the manners of society, it may be tolerated. So let us salute—and emulate—the cities on this list of Ten Best Mannered, including Council Bluffs, Iowa; Atlanta; Chicago; Los Angeles; Portland, Oregon; Rock Island-Moline, Ill.; Davenport-Bettendorf, Iowa; San Francisco; Denver; and Phoenix.

The geographical diversity of the list is impressive. So are the number of big cities mentioned—like Chicago and Atlanta and San Francisco. The presence of Chicago on the list is particularly assuring; it is too easy to assume that because a city is brawny ("Stormy, husky, brawling, / City of the big shoulders") it cannot be friendly. Chicago is. Always has been.

The cities on this list are an education to those of us who tend to assume, and presume, that manners are a holdover of the small-town South. We forget how widespread good manners still are, perhaps because so many of our visitors from other parts seem to consider our ways interesting artifacts of an earlier time—like birchbark canoes. We need to be reminded that manners, though they may be a Southern staple, are not a Southern monopoly.

In a classic essay on manners that appeared more than half a century ago, Stark Young reminded Southerners: "... we must re-member that we are concerned first with a quality itself, not as our own but as found anywhere; and that we defend certain qualities not because they belong to the South, but because the South belongs to them."

Manners may differ from place to place, from time to time, but they are anything but parochial. They are of the essence of any society. To quote Stark Young, "Manners and sincerity are matters understood only with reference to a state of society that assumes a group welfare and point of view rather than individual whims, a flow among a group of human beings, a life to which each single human being contributes and in which he lives."

Manners not only reflect a society; they create that society, which is why they should not only be recognized but taught. They are a way for the mass democracy that America has become to retain the dignity and deliberation of the Republic. In that sense, a set of manners shared and recognized by all is the most democratic *and* aristocratic of virtues. No one is more ill-mannered than the snob.

What do you suppose all these well-mannered cities will now do with their honor? Will Charleston (Heaven and the ghost of John C. Calhoun forbid) erect a billboard at the city limits proclaiming in flashing lights: "The Best Mannered City in the U.S.A."? Will its Chamber of Commerce put out a special mailing? Will someone suggest a tasteful way to boast? Will the federal government subsidize manners the way it does cotton and wheat, or sponsor a two-year study of Charleston with the aim of publishing a $3 million report on the care and cultivation of manners? You see the problem: How to celebrate manners, and so hope to inculcate them, without doing anything so vulgar as celebrating manners?

There ought to be a way. The future of American society depends on it, wouldn't you agree?

Modworld: Instant Tradition Arrives

The problem: People don't want to move into still another identical new subdivision and shop in still another identical new mall; what they crave in a place to live is diversity, tradition, and a human scale. What they don't want, to quote Patricia Leigh Brown in the *New York Times*, is one more string of "Red Barn Econolodges, 12-screen Cineplex Odeons or seamless subdivisions with 'Village' in their titles."

The solution: Instant tradition. Two designers—Andres Duany, 38, and his wife, Elizabeth Plater-Zyberg of Miami, Florida—propose to turn a 352-acre farm at Gaithersburg, Maryland, into a "planned village" of 1,600 residences. There will be 900,000 square feet of offices and a shopping center that will occupy another 1.2 million square feet. It'll have what the designers call a "grown up over time" feeling to be imposed by architecture and zoning. (Can't you almost see the ferns and taste the generic chablis now?)

What the designers say they don't want is another Reston, Virginia—a model community of another era—where Mr. Duany says "the automobile fragments the public experience." His approach would be different, he explains, skipping lightly over the one problem all such plans have in common: How can any place be both a model for the future and a community out of the past? It's akin to the problem of instant tradition, which tends to be as soul-satisfying as instant pudding.

What makes for the kind of cities Mr. Duany admires—those laid out sixty or seventy years ago around town squares—is that they have had sixty or seventy years to develop into communities from the model. No architectural layout or urban design has yet been found that can substitute for the unplanned workings of time and human intercourse.

For inspiration, these new designers take their team of architects, developers, builders, planners and city officials to old Annapolis, or to Georgetown in Washington, where they "share images, so when we refer to the feeling of a particular street we all know what we're talking about." In six days a new world is created on paper by three teams each going over the other's designs in brainstorming sessions, now called Charrettes. (Please pass the Rosé, now called Blush.)

The participants use a large-screen computer that can detail plans down to 1/100ths of an inch to get that old-time feeling. They take walks through the site in the moonlight to get a sense of place, and plug in their espresso machines for all-night sessions, yet never miss their obligatory, vitamin-filled breakfasts. Just reading about this Creative Process is enough to make a good ol' boy want to talk football while filling up on beer and pizza at the nearest smoke-filled bowling alley.

The whole approach brings to mind a slogan spotted on a teen-ager's button: "It's not who you are, it's what you wear." It's not how you live, it's what you live in that's supposed to deliver the old-time feelings of community, roots, continuity. Frank Lloyd Wright might not go for this recreation of the past but John Cheever would understand the desire. The whole venture is not about architecture so much as literature, or maybe sociology.

The planning team's finished product is a new design for an old village whose three neighborhoods are to span three centuries: farm buildings of Federal style, which is to federal as kosher is to kosher-style; a nineteenth-century street pattern; and a twentieth-century shopping center. This synthetic small town will be made mostly of traditional materials: brick, clapboard, and wood. It sounds like a really good exhibit in a museum, and doubtless will attract anybody who ever wanted to live in a really good exhibit in a museum. That's the usual result when architecture is used not as an expression of human history but as a substitute for it.

There's just one element, besides time, that the planners have overlooked. People. Maybe the designers could begin with a starter kit containing a few basic types native to any small town: The high school English teacher who has educated half the populace ("tough but fair; never played favorites"); the poor boy who went off and made good, then returned to endow a school or hand out meals at the Salvation Army; the inveterate entrepreneur who's always on the verge of making the deal that's going to leave him set for life, but somehow never does; the old shoemaker who still knows a vamp from a shank; the old family still feuding over some grievance whose origin is lost in antiquity; one each libertine and prude, miser and spendthrift, good ol' boy and good ol' girl; the retired nurse who spent 50 years in obstetrics and was the first to hold half the people she now knows; the merchant who's carried most of the town this side of the tracks when times were hard; selected characters from *It's a Wonderful Life*, a stock Andy, Aunt Bee, and Opie ....

What this Modworld in Maryland really needs is a little injection of Pine Bluff, Arkansas. Or Sherman, Texas. Or Paris, Tennessee. Then it might develop the full quota of solid citizens and ne'er-do-wells, civic leaders and public nuisances, rich and poor that every small town used to produce unremarked. Or would the poor and eccentric be planned out of a model community?

The final production, one suspects, would be less *Our Town* than *The Stepford Wives*. In comparison with this instantly traditional, good old Modworld, an ordinary strip development punctuated by Red Barn Econolodges, 12-screen Cineplex Odeons and seamless subdivisions might be refreshing.

Letter from the Other Place

(With Apologies to C.S. Lewis)

This communication was discovered in The Commercial *newsroom after a visit by a handsome, well-dressed young man with flashing eyes who affected red socks and an after-shave lotion that smelled slightly of sulphur and brimstone. If the young man would like the document back, we would be happy to return it by registered mail; there is no need for him to call for it in person.*

My dear Bluffpine,

Your favor of the 19th inst. has been gratefully received and duly recorded here in the home office. We were wondering where you would choose to open your practice and, while there is no doubt that you are the one to make that decision, being most familiar with conditions in the field, I would guard against over-optimism. You have a brilliant career ahead of you—if you will temper your enthusiasm with calculation, and moderate those fine theories you learned at the Institute of Satanic Technology with a little common sense. These small towns aren't as easy to crack as they may seem. (I know you get tired of hearing us old devils tell war stories, but did you ever hear about my exploits in Hadleyburg? It wasn't as easy as Mark Twain made it out to be.)

Your graphs and charts, and the statistics on poverty, unemployment, housing, and school drop-outs are impressive, but they don't go to the heart, or rather the soul, of the matter. You'll find this isn't like writing a term paper, and that the most impressive results can be obtained among the most affluent and learned members of the community, while the poor and seemingly ignorant have been known to foil even the most dedicated of tempters. Your reliance on racism, I'm afraid, is a bit old-fashioned in those latitudes. That old favorite isn't as potent as it once was. Try class prejudice; it's the coming thing.

I see you take great pride in turning the attention of those who are the objects of your snares away from public affairs and toward their private ones, believing you are creating civic apathy. Beware! Humans who concentrate on their children may soon enough develop an interest in the quality of the public schools, and there is no greater enemy of the divisions and discord you must sow. Let your clients become accustomed at an early age to working together, and learning and playing together, and they soon cease to be fit instruments of Our Satanic Father. And those humans who create successful businesses may soon enough be creating jobs for their fellows, or, Hell forbid, producing things of use and beauty. It is much better to steer them toward a generalized sloth. You know what they say about idle hands. Of course, if you can persuade them that they are much too good to take an interest in politics, that would be ideal. Politics offers the greatest possibilities for evil if only it can be reserved for the genuinely bad.

It seems to me you are much too fearful of the churches. For badness sake, don't waste your time and energy fretting about a church unless its members' conduct is actually influenced by what they hear there. It's what humans worship six days a week that counts. Nothing pleases me more than a great big empty cathedral. Unless it's a church crammed so full of petitions and prayers that there's no room for deeds. I would welcome more churches if they would all argue endlessly over theological differences in the most vehement fashion.

Don't confuse theology with religion; theology can be very useful. Remember the "religious" wars of the Middle Ages? Look at the great work being done in the Middle East and Northern Ireland. Get a theological dispute roaring and no telling what you can accomplish. Heavencloud and salvation, boy, don't start thinking of church people as lost to you, especially if they feel really superior. The self-righteous ones make the very best instruments for our work. Particularly useful are the sort who are convinced that their vocation is to criticize, and would never stoop to cooperating with their fellow, and lesser, creatures.

Superiority is an attitude definitely to be encouraged. Persuade enough humans that they're superior to the town they live in, and how under-appreciated they are by those around them, and you've got it made. I have found a solemn, self-satisfied superiority—beware any sign of humor!—to be the fastest route to these nether regions. Train humans to pay attention only to Their Own Kind, also called The Right Kind of People, and you'll find them following you quite complacently. Soon they'll be judging any idea on the basis of who proposes it, rather than its worth. Preferably, see that they have no ideas at all, and certainly no dissenting ones. This condition can be called Unity.

If your clients do show signs of wanting to do something for the town or their fellows, by all means divert them from actually helping each other. Keep them busy trying to impress others, preferably by erecting some elaborate facade that will consume all their energy and resources. This can be called Progress. (Remember Babel?) Elaborate civic ceremonies make particularly attractive diversions. Let them concentrate on ways to improve their "image" just so long as they don't try to improve anything else.

Above all, make certain your subjects discuss anything negative in only the most positive way, if at all. And soon they'll be very pleased with themselves. Or, which is just as good, make them disillusioned and very sorry for themselves, convinced that the place is hopeless. Either way, the town will be well on its way to resembling these nice warm quarters.

Beware of those types who insist on doing what good they can for others regardless of reward. They're the insidious ones. Keep telling them they're fools for working for nothing. If they must do good, see that they do it for some kind of compensation—money, status, power—rather than the good itself. When the reward disappears, so may their inclination to earn it. What plans do you have to discourage all the volunteer work done in the community? That would seem your biggest challenge. I must tell you the head office is most concerned about your failure to make progress in this area.

This is important: Encourage secrecy and cliques. Beware open discussion and any sense of community; few things can hurt our chances more. Divide and conquer, and soon you'll be promoted. I understand there's an opening in Kansas City for an accomplished young devil. (Houston and Dallas are already in competent hands.) But if you don't do something about those blasted volunteers, and good neighbors, and understanding friends, you're going to find yourself demoted to some dingy bar in North Little Rock.

One more thing: Have your people get in the habit of pouring unwarranted praise on each other. Nothing so devalues the real, deserved thing. I wouldn't put too much effort in this systematic plan of yours to delegate mischief-making. Take it from an old timer: Nothing works any better than personally going to and fro in the land. Keep up the bad work, let us hear of your progress, and never underestimate the Enemy. He is cunning as a serpent, gentle as a dove, and can insinuate good into even the worst of them. They'll fool you, so keep your guard up!

Your ever watchful superior,
Tapescrew

Small Towns: Who Will Save Them?

To paraphrase what Leo Tolstoy said about families, happy small towns are all alike; every unhappy one is unhappy in its own way. A recent conference on the American small town at, appropriately enough, Grinnell College in Grinnell, Iowa, indicates that the American small town is alive and, if not well, hanging on gamely. That's good to hear, because one suspects that, as small towns go, so does America.

Perhaps the only disturbing thought on reading of a conference on small town life is that this country may honor certain social institutions only when they're about to disappear. The air of nostalgia that hovers over such gatherings may be pleasant, but nostalgia generally concerns the past, not the future.

The small towns of Iowa, too, sound like poetry when recited: Cheer, Hawkeye, Morning Sun, Lone Tree, Gravity, Defiance...though they seem to lack some of the nutty zest and sheer Southern grandiloquence of Arkansas names: Alabam, Arkadelphia, Bald Knob, Bright Star, Ben Hur, Birdsong, Calico Rock, Greasy Corner, Jenny Lind, Morning Star, Rosebud, Urbanette (rhymes with Grapette), Strawberry, Shady Grove (Arkansas has two of those), Velvet Ridge, Whisp, Yancopin, Pine Bluff (which we like to think of as an honorary small town even if it's become a small city), and, just about my favorite, Tarry. As in "Tarry a while..." Little Rock would be a great name if it were still attached to a small town instead of having been swallowed up by a whole metropolitan area. Much like the lovely name Philadelphia.

If Grinnell is any example, small towns have not changed much, which is encouraging. Thomas Rawls wrote a piece about the conference for *Harrowsmith* magazine out of Charlotte, Virginia, and he tells about his reception in Grinnell: "I'm standing on the corner of

Fourth and Broad in Grinnell, Iowa, and generally gawking. As I look things over, in apparent befuddlement, a kindly woman inquires: 'You look confused. Can I help you?' 'Oh, uh, no, thank you,' I reply, because however confused I appear, I am no more puzzled than usual. I'm just taking in the scenery. Then as I amble up Broad Street on an unseasonably warm day, the first two people I pass on the sidewalk smile and say hello. They don't merely nod or mutter an unintelligible greeting; they offer a genuine salutation."

Sounds a lot like Pine Bluff, or certainly what Pine Bluff used to be and still, thankfully, often is—a place where a greeting is still a greeting and not a cursory half-smile and ambiguous sound. Where people's eyes still meet, that's a small town. The first rule on the New York subway is never to engage anyone else's eyes; it might set up a human relationship, with all its terrifying possibilities.

At Grinnell, the symposium on small-town life is full of good memories. Distinguished speaker after distinguished speaker remembers growing up in a small town and asserts that's what growing up should be like. Why? To quote Mr. Rawls, "Boys and girls grow up in a mingling of rich and poor, in a place where, to make things work, people must participate. They move among adults who know them and learn what it takes to earn their respect." As one speaker at the conference puts it, "You see how everything works. You can understand the whole system."

The object of all the striving in the country's great megaplexes seems to be to get away from the poor. That being impossible in a small town, people tend to concentrate on better things. The small town is the world in microcosm. Institutions like the church, the public school system, the boys' club, all play their part in this process of *E Pluribus Unum*. The number of American leaders produced by small towns isn't just a cherished myth; it's a statistical finding. Try to think of American presidents who came from large cities; you can count them on the fingers of one hand and have two or three fingers left over.

One troubling aspect of conferences like Grinnell's is that the distinguished leaders who recall their youth so fondly on these occasions aren't likely to live in small towns now that they're distinguished leaders. There are some glorious exceptions, but it's assumed that the best and brightest will move on and up.

Paul Gruchow, a writer from Worthington, Minnesota, calls that assumption "one of the central themes of small-town life," and tells a story that will ring true to every small-towner: When a hometown boy was involved in a murder elsewhere, the townspeople rallied to defend him, and started looking for a good lawyer. Paul Gruchow's wife happens to be a defense attorney of some experience and expertise. So one night he gets a phone call from a fellow townsman asking if he knows a good lawyer in *Minneapolis*.

The classic small-town inferiority complex seems to remain the same whether you're in Worthington, Minnesota, or Pine Bluff, Arkansas. We don't give ourselves enough credit, which may explain both the apathy and boosterism that seem to alternate in small towns. The sociologists have accepted the American small town as a remarkable place ever since the Lynds did their landmark study of Muncie, Indiana, in the 1920s, but the people who live there may never have come to terms with their own quality. That absence of self-consciousness, sometimes even self-awareness, makes small towns revealing even at their supposed dullest.

Forget all the leaders that small towns are supposed to produce for the rest of America, and consider only the village atheist, the town eccentric, the lone aginner. Each has a character all his own that their city cousins lack. Perhaps the solitary nature of their calling in a small town explains it; their idiosyncrasies are not diluted by having to be shared with masses of nonconformists.

It would be hard to imagine William Faulkner or Maxwell Anderson writing as they did about great cities, or Thomas Wolfe celebrating America as he did if he had come from any place larger than Asheville, North Carolina. There is a special, personal quality about the small-towner—whether leader or freethinker, conformist or non—

that comes with the limited territory, and that only the lucky few may be able to find in Bigcity, U.S.A.

Now there is a new interest in the American small town—and conferences on the subject. But something tells me that conferences and everything that goes with them—master plans, sociologese, federal grants—will be of peripheral use in saving whatever quality it is that draws us to small towns. Social planning may be able to produce an unreasonable facsimile of a small town, an architectural style, a big city on a small scale—but not the genuine article. Bureaucracy has its benefits, but it never produced a soul. You can no more create an instant small town than you can create instant history or instant character.

All help will be gratefully accepted, but in the end small towns will have to be saved by the people who live there. And isn't that part of small-town wisdom? Weren't you always told that there are some things nobody can do for you?

Lost on the Freeway

DALLAS—He was like an ex-husband talking about why he had been attracted to his wife, and how things had gone sour. He was both angry and wistful. Only this old boy was talking about the city he loved and couldn't stop talking about, and now just wanted out of: "This place has changed. It used to be run by people with character. Sure, it was a screwy character sometimes and the old crowd was often wrong, but it was never uncertain. As for the ones in charge of things now—They Are Not Nice People. I'm not even sure they're people; they're sure not folks.

They're more like animated balance sheets. They have no passion except for aggrandizement. As the buildings got higher, the people got smaller. The old cowboy culture has given way to lizard boots and glitz. Oh, the old Dallas may still be there somewhere under it all, maybe over in Fort Worth, but you can't see it from the executive suite. They keep taking my perks away and that's supposed to make me feel real bad; they don't understand that I just want to be left alone to do my work, and the fewer limos and lunches I have to fool with, the happier I am. They think I'm like them."

Although I've made only sporadic visits to Dallas over the years, I think I understand what he was talking about. Every time I come through, the airport is more of a hassle, the office buildings more jarringly disparate (and emptier), and the freeways more homicidal. It is the freeways that most impress and depress. Years ago I was taken to the top of a revolving restaurant here to be shown the glory and grandeur that awaited in Dallas. The time was chosen with some premeditation—nightfall, as the city came aglow far below. But what stood out was the interminable, intersecting interstates and the commuting time each represented. The whole city had been dissected and malformed for the purpose of getting out of it at high speed.

It was not really an urban scene at all but a vast suburban sprawl, centerless, amorphous, circling. Every 45 minutes our table at the Chez Centrifugal passed the one familiar, fatal spot in the panorama: the Texas Book Depository. Now someone has made a museum out of it by building a sleek elevator shaft that takes visitors directly, comfortably, speedily to the room Lee Harvey Oswald used that November day to blight history. There is no need to climb up flights of stairs or feel the oppressive weight of the past; it is a kind of freeway to history.

Individually, the buildings that come bolting by the freeways might hold some interest. There is a replica of the Crystal Palace that would be a thing to contemplate if one had more time and space than are available in Dallas. But the Crystal Palace flashes by along-side Victorian revivals, French chateaux, banks that look like churches and churches that look like banks, faceless slabs given new angles in the vain hope of making them appear other than faceless slabs. . . .

The whole architectural catalogue is flipped through at upwards of 55 miles per hour. Assorted images speed past like the carved steeds of a dizzying carousel, in the end all blending into one vague flash. It could as well be the center of Oklahoma City or the outreaches of Atlanta's big bang. All across the South, the country towns disappear and the old cities are encrusted with the usual alien life forms till the sum total of all this distinctive architecture is the same indistinctive swirl.

In Dallas, the front porch was replaced long ago by high rises—and high rollers. The lead story in this Sunday's edition of the *Times Herald* begins: "A task force of federal prosecutors and FBI agents is seizing financial records of at least 290 Texas developers and savings and loan executives in an investigation into suspected crimes that sparked a crisis in the state's S&L industry and could cost the federal thrift insurance fund up to $3 billion. Documents obtained by . . ."

The scope of Texican ambitions and how far they can ripple is scarcely news to anybody from Pine Bluff, Ark., where one of the largest federally insured savings-and-loan ever to fold had made extensive investments in Dallas real estate. The optimists say it'll take five years, maybe ten, for the Dallas market to recover but, despite a vacancy rate estimated at 30 percent, construction goes on all around as if by some involuntary reflex. Each empty new building would be a landmark if there were not so many of them. Instead, they huddle together like monuments in a crowded cemetery.

The other, older Dallas has been driven underground, or maybe to Fort Worth. Friends here talk about Fort Worth in a tone reserved for a last redoubt of reality. The old East Texas ways live on, quietly and uncelebrated except in the loser's lyrics of country songs and the looks of people who still work for a living.

In Pine Bluff the week before, an old classmate of my wife's had dropped in to catch up on the last 20 years. We took him out to Jones Cafe for catfish and cornbread and sweet potato pie, and found that he had married a Japanese American. He told us one of her family stories—about how her grandfather, eager to become Americanized, had left the West Coast and settled in a small town in Louisiana back in the 1920s. As a photographer, the immigrant's chief source of income was the nearby army base, where he took pictures of the recruits—the kind they could send the folks back home. When Pearl Harbor came, the FBI sent word to the sheriff that the Japanese photographer, with his easy access to a military installation, would have to be arrested and interned.

The sheriff knew the family, had known it for a long time. He said that if the old man had to be arrested, the FBI would have to get past him first. The family remained unmolested in the shade of the army camp during the war years. The old man's children and his children's children grew into the usual productive citizens that fill the ranks of Japanese Americans. (Our friend's wife was a physician.) And all because one single, stubborn redneck would not lend himself to the hysteria whose writ ran from Washington to the West Coast.

The morning after our visitor had left, a priest appeared in my office. He said he was looking the town over and asked what Pine Bluff was like. I told him it was a place where people had roots, that it had changed a lot in the last quarter of a century, like so much of the South, and that there was still much to be done—historic buildings to be saved, a symphony to be started, schools to be supported, jobs to be created...I added that the town was still of such a scale that here a single individual could make a great difference. The priest seemed to understand; he said he had been reared in a city this size but was now ministering in a suburb of one of the country's great sprawling metropolises. He mentioned that his average congregant stayed with the church about six years before moving on.

That conversation came back to me in Dallas when we visited an old friend and lunched on bagels and some smoked salmon from the batch he had caught on a Canadian fishing trip. The Dallas Symphony, he hinted, was not up to New York standards. After lunch he invited me along to his exercise spa but the most vigorous exertion I had in mind was a brisk nap. I was leaning back and admiring his swimming pool around which the house and gardens were built when I heard my host ask the inevitable question: "What is there to *do* in Pine Bluff?"

v | THE SOUTH

What Is the South?

NEW ORLEANS—"What's the South like?" said the man in the white suit. "That's what they all ask. Which South do you mean—the ante-bellum mansion, the fly-specked roadhouse, or that latest of the New Souths, the Sunbelt? Or one of the uncountable other Souths? And which image is the facade for which? Do not be quick to decide. It is not easy to see which culture is supplanting the other. The professional Southerner may turn out to be all leaf and no roots; the most Southern of us all may never think on what it means to be Southern."

He paused to sip at his mint julep. "Actually, I prefer Scotch. The South is the unswerving preservation of tradition on selected occasions. The South is the Natchez Trace, that dream highway meandering through forests only as deep as the right-of-way, with faithful old retainers posted at convenient distances to guide and refresh, and assure us that all is as it seems. It's a high road that rises up green and lush beyond every curve and over every rise. The South is Highway 61 that runs right alongside the Trace, featuring misspelled signs and abandoned drive-in movie theaters. It's grass growing through the cracks of an abandoned concrete parking lot. New dreams here fade before the old ones do. To be Southern is to want nothing more than to live by the side of the road and board up the windows to outsiders.

"The South is driving along a Mississippi back road in the dead heat of a hot Sunday afternoon while listening to a black preacher on the radio praising the Lord in half song, half sermon—as close as contemporary man can come to the original spirit of the Psalms. Logically, it would seem easier to say grace over oysters Rockefeller and trout meunière at Galatoire's than over potlikker and biscuits with Hoover Gravy, but of course it is the other way around in the South, as elsewhere. The South is no longer Christ-centered, if it ever was, but it is still Christ-fixated; even the oh-so-rational Deists seem to have a bitter edge of fervor to their denials. It would take a Dostoyevsky to understand us; we sure can't, though we never cease confidently explaining ourselves to one another. Walker Percy said it: 'The Southerner started out a skeptical Jeffersonian and became a crooked Christian. That is to say, he is approaching and has almost reached his essence, which is to be more crooked and Christian than ever before. Do you want a portrait of the New Southerner? He is Billy Graham on Sunday and Richard Nixon the rest of the week.' "

The man in the white suit punctuated his quotation with a sip and doubtful smile, then continued: "Perhaps Dostoyevsky would not know us, after all. Potemkin would. We are determined to save our priceless heritage if the price is right. The Southern ideal is the classical one—of harmony, completeness, evenness. Our *beau ideal* is not the tortured and agonized existential hero, or the witty and ambitious leader at the top of the greasy pole, but the whole man. Our ideal is the man without a mark on him, the woman in the portraits. Our hero is Robert E. Lee, not Abe Lincoln. The Southerner must be all of a piece, unthinking except in tactics and manners—all one unmarred piece of alabaster. No wonder we break under the strain of living up to such a specification.

"Our idea of the good has come to be the simple, the whole, so instinctively understandable as not to require explication, at least not in words. That would be to desecrate it, like cracking a piece of marble. The Southerner aims for a literal integrity. Perhaps that is why we keep producing the partial, the incomplete, the unnatural, and explicating them to death. Flannery O'Connor, as usual, explained it: 'Whenever I'm asked why Southern writers particularly have a penchant for writing about freaks, I tell them you have to have some conception of the whole man.'

"The key to that wholeness is the past. It is the only thing that lasts. 'The past is never dead,' said Faulkner. 'It is not even past.' Though it lingers longer in some places than others—like here in New Orleans and in the nameless little cotton towns one passes through on the way to someplace else. But there is no escaping it even along the franchise rows, in the midst of the industrial parks, even next to the air conditioning vents. We are the only part of the country to have been defeated explicitly, and defeat lasts longer than victory and in some ways is sweeter. Whether we learned anything from defeat and occupation is problematic; we were not so much instructed as fascinated by the experience. Its effect has been not cautionary but romantic. The politicians we honor are not the most effective or successful, but the dreamiest. How else explain the worship of Jefferson Davis?

"Most of all, we hate the politician who can see a little further than most and commits the indiscretion of telling the rest of us about it. We cast him into obloquy as soon as he betrays any sign of prescience. The only reason we still honor John C. Calhoun, who may have been the most far-sighted of them all, is that we have confused that hardbitten realist with a romantic dreamer.

"Southernism itself is a curious, alien patriotism, the product of both America and of the separate nation we were for four long, arduous years, perhaps longer. We are still a different country in the important, informal ways that are the most enduring. The honorable Southerner, like General Lee and Admiral Semmes, is still on parole, sincerely wishing to live up to the terms of his pardon, but without violating some interior honor. That produces an interesting tension. The Southerner is tempted to make up for his slightly subversive past by bouts of star-spangled jingoism that are not very convincing, or lasting.

"What's the South? It is a reflection in an assortment of fragmented mirrors—some warped, others beveled and tarnished, some much too clear for comfort, still others made of plastic. And there is no way to tell which is the sure image. The best course is to depend on none of them, but to approach the subject without preconceived or received ideas, which, for a Southerner, is an impossibility."

A streetcar whirred and clanged by in the distance and the haze of the day grew steamier. A tray of beignets and café au lait caught my attention. When I turned back, the man in the white suit was gone. Only his empty glass remained—palpable, shimmering, waiting to be filled again and again. Like the South.

Think Pink

What was once common currency this time of year becomes increasingly rare as tomato season arrives. The Bradley County Pink, the official fruit *and* vegetable of Arkansas, has become the latest victim of all-American merchandising. By a kind of Gresham's Law of tomatoes, the pink is being driven into rarity by nice but unexceptional varieties like Mountain Pride and Mountain Delight. These mountain reds are selling tomatoes; the Arkansas pink is an *eating* tomato, and there is a vast difference.

Like certain fine wines, the Arkansas pink does not travel well. Nor does it have the bright red color and squared-off look that characterize the modern industrial tomato, which is designed for packing crates rather than for palates. The reds have all the durability of a small softball, and about as much taste. The pink began to fade from Bradley County and thereabouts over the past decade. It remains evident in the name of the Bradley County Pink Tomato Festival, which it now graces largely in absentia.

Apparently there is no product however fine that cannot be

improved to the point of non-recognition by modern techniques. The modern American supermarket tomato-and-doorstop has been geneticized, chemicalized, sanitized and Simonized till it looks like the glossiest, high-quality photograph of a tomato—and has about as much taste. Its heft is uniform but unsatisfying, its aroma plastic, and its innards appear pre-frozen on even the hottest day. The essential function of this substitute tomato is visual rather than gustatory. Calvin Trillin of *The New Yorker* magazine and one of the country's great eaters rather than a mere gourmet, warned some years back that anyone throwing one of these modern tomatoes would "risk being arrested for assault to kill."

The mod tomato attains its glossy, skin-deep beauty by being picked rock hard before being exposed to ethylene gas. Then it is transported across the continent to the tables of innocents who have grown up thinking of tomatoes as a nice but tasteless garnish. In exchange for its luscious color, the modern heavy-duty tomato loses only its scent, taste, juicy texture, and soul. The more processed variety may not only be gassed in violation of the Geneva Convention but soaked in a brine that has been treated with carbon dioxide. That way, the victims can be kept fresh, or rather mummified, for months or even years. Sometimes the mummies are coated in wax. Often they're taken directly home from the supermarket to be put in the *refrigerator*, for goshsakes. If they had any taste before, it would be killed by that final indignity.

The fate that has befallen the tomato in modern times is but another entry in that well-known department, Worse Things Through Chemistry. P. J. Wingate, who worked for Du Pont for years, once explained why folks keep buying these simulacra: "For about 10 months each year most people in the U.S. eat thin slices of a red colored fruit (or vegetable) which are almost as tough and tasteless as so many slices from one of those new orange golf balls. People keep on eating these rubbery red slices partly from habit but mostly because they remember how good vine-ripened tomatoes were last August, and they keep hoping that some of the golf balls being shipped in from Florida, California and Mexico will have that same taste. They never do. Then when hope has just begun to be abandoned, the real tomato returns and begins a two-month campaign to restore its reputation.''

That restorative campaign begins right here in Arkansas with the Bradley Country Pink Tomato Festival, or at least it used to when the first lugs of pinks would appear in their own good time. It may be another week or two before this delight is ready for picking (there's been a lot of rain this year) but you can still find the species if you really look.

It would be an atrocity to let a Bradley County Pink see the inside of a refrigerator. It belongs on a window sill silently awaiting the arrival of perfection as it continues to ripen off the vine, although a little Vivaldi or Mozart is permitted. Please, no jarring Beethoven. Willie Nelson singing old favorites *sotto voce* probably wouldn't hurt, although this last is a help mainly in ripening the *eater*. The Bradley County Pink has a sensitive nervous system and there are cases reported of some being absolutely petrified by Jerry Lee Lewis.

The genuine Arkansas pink tomato should never be eaten without taking a moment to notice one of nature's finest works. Pause to let the law of gravity bring home its just-right weight. Note how this tomato was designed not for shipping purposes but for the human palm. This fruit has no need of gas, brine, wax and fine wrapping paper. It just sits there and blushes, the way the naturally good do. This is the future come into its own at last, the fruit of patience. It is tangible, palatable proof of the goodness of time, and the folly of trying to rush it or hold it back. This is a fruit that need not shout or shine, but only be.

What we have in the de-evolution of the American tomato (the name comes from the Aztec *tomatl*) is not really a triumph of American marketing but a failure to market the right product. Here in Arkansas, we have the Vidalia Onion of the tomato world, yet it is fast becoming an endangered species commercially. Instead of letting the Bradley County Pink become a local secret, it should be shared with all those starved for the real thing. A market has been developed for even canned, organically grown tomatoes. Imagine what Arkansas's ambrosial product might command if only it could be brought safely to a waiting world at a modest but remunerative

rofit. (But what could we buy half so precious as that we sold?)
There are dozens of ways to fix tomatoes. Ratatouille. The classic
:on-lettuce-and-tomato sandwich. Or a simple tomato and mayonnaise
s dwich on white bread consumed early in the season over the
kit en sink. Bruschetti. (That's crusty, toasted or grilled bread slices
rubbed with garlic, topped with tomato slices, sprinkled with a little
olive oil.) But the best recipe for tomato remains:

Take one perfectly ripened Bradley County Pink. (Ingredients are
all in these matters.) Hold it up to the light, feel its heft, enjoy its
scent, appreciate its color and slightly erratic contours. Then, using a
very sharp knife, slice thin on a wooden board, and eat, savoring every
bite. If you must, add just a little coarse salt—just a little, a suspicion
of a pinch, no more. It's not the taste of the salt you're after. Or you
might want to serve the slices between two pieces of good black
bread, unaccompanied. One taste and you know summer is here.

Apologia Pro Redneck

It is reported with a straight face that one Harold Smith, president of
the local historical society in Smyrna, Ga., will lead an effort to get
the National Geographic to apologize for using the term "redneck"
to describe his town.

Can the gentleman from Smyrna be under the impression that
redneck is a term of opprobrium rather than an estate, like matrimony,
to be honored and preserved? If so, he is laboring under a delusion
that has grown common even this side of Mason-Dixon's Line. To
quote Kathryn Jensen, the author of the best one-volume guide to
redneckin' that I know (*Redneckin'*, Putnam, 1983)—"...we know

some folks hold that redneck ain't a particular nice name for a body. Well, we don't agree. When you're a redneck, things is a lot more simple and satisfyin'. Your basic redneck is just common folk livin' common style and tryin' the best he can to get along the best he can. Redneckin' is enjoyin' the simple things in life, workin' hard, not a-lettin' yourself be bothered by a heap a hard questions and worrisome ideas, and raisin' a little hell ever now and then. It's eatin' good ol' American food, dressin' in a way that looks and feels good, dancin', drivin' a truck, and the like."

Redneck is just another name for no-airs, and if the gentleman from Smyrna would think about which he'd rather see when stranded by the side of the road with a flat tire or a busted fan belt—a yuppie with P.H.S. (Perfect Hair Syndrome) whizzing past in his BMW or a good ol' boy chugging along in an old pickup with a gun rack and time to spare for his fellow man—well, he might come to realize that redneck is an encomium, not an insult.

As usual, the nicefiers of the language would deprive us not only of an honest word but of what it stands for. If they are allowed their way, and the redneck becomes unmentionable in the National Geographic and other artifacts of polite society, the concept itself may have to go. What a loss that would be, not just to the language but to the region.

What would replace the redneck—some neutral, indistinct, colorless species too bland to have a name? A sort of imitation Yankee? H. L. Mencken summed up that new type some time ago in his masterpiece of vitriol, "The Sahara of Bozart," when he referred to "third-rate Southerners inculcated with the worst traits of the Yankee sharper." His essay is still remembered as a classic assault on Southern culture (or what was left of it in the '20s), but its most perceptive line often is overlooked: "The Southerner, at his worst, is never the surly cad that the Yankee is."

The relationship between the redneck and the Southern gentleman is not an easy one; it might be described as an amiable antipathy. Each half-envies, half-despises, and is wholly tempted to imitate the other on occasion, the way two different halves of a whole may complement yet compete with the other. It would take a Faulkner to plumb the depth of this uneasy relationship. He might do it in a single sentence, but the rest of us tend to stumble and mutter around the edges, knowing that the difference between redneck and gentleman not only separates but unites the two, and that it would be a grave error to dismiss the term redneck as a simple insult instead of shorthand for a complicated social code.

Rednecks celebrate simplicity as a welcome change from a fraudulent sophistication, yet that scarcely makes them simple. The code of the redneck is as involved as any planter's or bedouin's, and a good deal trickier than that of the modern urbanite who lives by the motto *Regnat Pecunia*. Whatever the redneck is, he shares with the gentleman the essence of what he is not: He is not modern. And so he is bound to be condemned by those who are.

In their uncorrupted state, the redneck and the gentleman share a common indifference to the great pantheon of mod gods—Success, Progress, Power, the Bottom Line—and that is what makes each a deeply subversive influence in modern civilization, or what passes for it. Both are endangered species. Modernity conspires to make redneck a bad word and merchandise Lady and Gentleman as synonyms for woman and man. The classic types are as much at home in this newest of the New Souths as Confucius would be in today's collectivized China. They epitomize an older culture and so are anathema to those who would modernize it.

The status of a name can be a fair indication of the morale of the people who go by it. Another quintessential Southern group once had to labor under the term Negro or Colored rather than black. When a culture is thought to require a euphemism, it is well on its way to being lost. When a good, simple word is restored, so are the people it describes. The first step to losing the redneck would be to lose the word, and that would be a sad loss, no matter what the oh-so-respectable among us may think; they have been misled by a snobbism masquerading as gentility.

Those who object to the term redneck might as well take offense at Arkie or Okie, black or Creole. The Southern language already has lost enough distinctive words to the bowdlerizers and euphemizers; let's not lose one that sums up a whole ethos.

In Defense of Manners

There are some frills that are not frills but are of the essence. They are mistaken for frills only by those ignorant of their significance. That is what seems to have happened to manners.

The manners of a society are its hallmark, its glue, its ritual, the medium in which it thrives or withers. To the thoughtless, manners are superficial; to the thoughtful, they reveal the substance of a society. In a culture as diverse as this one, they make it possible for very different people to live together in mutual consideration. Even more important, they make it possible for people to preserve their individual differences by adopting a common code that shields all. Manners are tolerance codified, patience embodied, kindness made the standard in small things so that it may grow to govern the great ones. Manners are the outward fruition of an inner discipline. Valuable in themselves, they provide an invaluable example in other realms of thought and conduct.

Manners give all permission to be kind, freeing us to do our best for each other. Manners should not constrict but open personalities, in the way a common language guides all its speakers to new and eloquent heights. Manners make us self-conscious in the best way; they can make a small act a great one, and make great acts delicate ones. The best manners are not rigid but the instruments of a happy and gracious flexibility.

Manners are also boundaries, the kind only barbarians transgress ignorantly. A gentleman has been defined as someone who would never insult another unintentionally. Manners are an example of the kind of restraint that frees, which is part of their mystery.

But this is an age not receptive to mystery. There must be a rationale, preferably practical, for the beautiful, the kind, the restorative. The headline over a story about teaching manners at a local elementary school reads: "Good Manners Can Make One More Attractive and Liked"—which has the ring of "Honesty Is the Best

Policy." As if the intrinsic worth of a practice had to be justified by some good result. Art for practicality's sake.

Very well. There is no end of good reasons for manners: They are an eloquent means of communication, a highly efficient way of doing things, and a steadying reminder that we are all civilized here and intend to remain so. They are a way of putting each other at ease and, when necessary, not too much at ease. They are both emblem and essence of society, region, culture, family—all of which they under-gird and broaden. That is why it should be of particular concern to a society, a region, a culture, or a family when manners fade or are never learned. Not just a legacy is being lost but a future. Manners are a thing of beauty *and* use.

Manners are an art as well as a science, an applied art that consists of more than the sum of its rules. Who has the best manners? The one who best puts the rest of the company at ease, according to one old standard.

Manners are the sacraments of society, focusing attention on the ordinary and so elevating it to the extraordinary, hallowing the mundane. They are perhaps the best evidence of Thomas Jefferson's theory about a natural aristocracy among humanity. I have seen cowboys around a campfire, a slightly drunken peasant in a Mexican border town, a harassed waitress in a beer joint, a field hand by the side of the road...all display manners that can only be described as exquisite, and, yes, I've also seen the well dressed and well coiffed Upwardly Mobile act like louts. To see in which direction a society is headed, there may be a better guide than the laws it passes, or even the songs it sings: the manners it practices. As Wallace Stevens said of mythology, manners do more than reflect the region that produces them; they are of its sub-stance, "wood out of its forest..."

All of this is why it was assuring to read about the volunteer in the Pine Bluff public school system who is teaching manners to second graders at Forrest Park. Behind all the rules in the Good Manners restaurant inaugurated in that classroom, there is a history, a purpose, a way of life. In the Good Manners restaurant, gentlemen open doors for ladies, rise when ladies enter a room, and let ladies go first.

No one eats till all are served and, very important, voices are lowered in conversation so that those at nearby tables are not disturbed.

Perhaps if all students received this kind of attention in the second grade, more schools could avoid the barbaric practice of forbidding conversation in the cafeteria during mealtimes. It's called Quiet Time, a euphemism for Shaddup Time, and is said to be practiced a couple of times a week in some local schools—right here in Pine Bluff, in what is left of The South. This sort of thing, which is only one small symptom of the new barbarism, won't be extirpated simply by expressing horror. It will have to be replaced by something better, like civilized conversation. That institution and recreation is coming back, at least in one grade of one school.

Let's hope the rebirth of manners will spread throughout the school system and far beyond—the way fresh green grass will in fertile Southern soil—if it is nourished and weeded. The sight of these students and teachers bringing back civilization is enough to renew the rest of us. Thank you.

Name Your Book

What a nice way for a Southern magazine to celebrate its silver anniversary. Isie Peat of *Southern Living* has sent me a survey form with spaces for my 10 favorite works of Southern literature. The results of the survey are to appear soon and, as soon as they do, I know I'll clasp a hand to my forehead and go, "Of course! How could I have forgotten that one!"

What a pleasure to answer Isie Peat's letter. And what a splendid excuse for an essay, since I'm supposed to comment on my top three choices. This is the kind of assignment that makes an inky wretch of the press think he should be paying the boss. Let's see how many of my choices would be yours.

(1) Faulkner, of course. But which book? *Light in August* is my favorite. I can still remember reading it for the first time, and turning down the pages I wanted to re-read and savor. That lasted for about the first four, five, six pages till it became clear that they were all like that.

Faulkner captured and thereby recreated not just a city, as Lawrence Durrell did Alexandria and Naguib Mahfouz Cairo, but a region, a legacy, a state of mind. He made a world everlasting into a book, into a sentence. He captured the South *and* evoked her. He concentrated *and* expanded a world.

How did he do it? How did he make of fervor and memory and music his and our truth? The saving truth of Faulkner forms the first sentences of Chapter Six of *Light in August*: "Memory believes before knowing remembers. Believes longer than recollects, longer than knowing even wonders...." If there is still to be a South, if the faith is kept, memory will be why.

I would choose Faulkner because his world was and became ours, and because every Southern writer since has tried to do what he did: frame the perfect sentence, the one wave that would explain all the others.

What makes a sentence Faulknerian? Its ambition, of course, its grasp for a whole universe, but also its hunger—its hunger for old words unheard for years, for ages. Suddenly they appear in just the right order, like a complete silver service with strange pieces whose use is a mystery, dug up where it had been buried in the summer of 1864, and recalled to perfectly serviceable life.

(2) I led my list with *Light in August* because its Christmas story reminds me of another favorite author: Flannery O'Connor. She knew Southern literature could not be the same after Faulkner. In a sense it became Southern literature *only* after him. T. S. Eliot, who was a better critic than a poet, said that "what happens

when a new work of art is created is something that happens simultaneously to all the works of art which preceded it." He understood that the past was "attuned by the present as much as the present is directed by the past." Or as Flannery O'Connor explained in one of her essays: "The presence alone of Faulkner in our midst makes a great difference in what the writer can and cannot permit himself to do. Nobody wants his mule and wagon stalled on the same track the Dixie Limited is roaring down."

But which book of Miss O'Connor's would one choose? It would have to be a collection of short stories. Being a newspaper columnist and obliged to follow politics, the story I find applicable almost daily is "Enoch and the Gorilla," with its perfect, unspoken elucidation of the assumption that all you need do is slip on the right persona and the world is yours. Enoch Emery required only a gorilla suit; other folks are more demanding but the principle is the same. I don't want to shock anybody, but Enoch's assumption is not limited to politicians. It is not unknown even among newspaper columnists.

In her essays, Flannery O'Connor says the obvious—but it wasn't obvious until she said it. Asked why Southern writers all seem to write about freaks, she pointed out that it was because, in the South, we can still tell a freak when we see one. I am not sure that is still true. I know I want it to be. It took a Flannery O'Connor to see that "anything that comes out of the South is going to be called grotesque by the Northern reader, unless it is grotesque, in which case it is going to be called realistic."

It was she who summed up the current and maybe permanent Southern dilemma: "The anguish that most of us have observed for some time now has been caused not by the fact that the South is alienated from the rest of the country, but by the fact that it is not alienated enough, that every day we are getting more and more like the rest of the country, that we are being forced out not only of our many sins, but of our few virtues."

(3) Douglas Southall Freeman's monumental biography of Robert E. Lee. For balance. For the alabaster code that rises above all else,

even and especially defeat. For the Richmond editor's appreciation of Lee as much as for Lee himself. Because when Robert E. Lee ceases to be appreciated, the South will be merely the past and not what it is: history. There *is* a difference between the two, just as there is a difference between one's environment and one's world. I would choose Freeman's biography of Lee for the pagan, stoic virtues that are at the center of the South, despite the few pious imprecations he throws in toward the end.

How fill out this list of 10? Robert Penn Warren's *All the King's Men,* a must for aficionados of Southern politics, particularly its Mediterranean aspects. *The Moviegoer* by Walker Percy—in order to pay one's respects to Dr. Percy and modern anomie, Southern fried. There should be room on the list for snapshots of the Southern mentality at different epochs, and from different views: W. J. Cash's *The Mind of the South* and the lesser, more sociological treatise, *Caste and Class in a Southern Town* by John Dollard. *Up From Slavery* by Booker T. Washington to demonstrate that there is a thread of sanity in the Southern character—and to do justice to the most underrated (at least among capital-I Intellectuals) of Southern leaders.

Then would come either U. B. Phillips's *Life and Labor in the Old South* or the Agrarians' manifesto, *I'll Take My Stand.* Either would show how we were—and therefore, being Southerners, how we still are. Finally, James Agee's *Let Us Now Praise Famous Men*—though it, too, acquires a dated sound.

What books would you add? I am only two chapters into *The Oldest Living Confederate Widow* by Alan Gurganus, and already wondering if it belongs on the list. And where is Eudora Welty's *The Ponder Heart?* How about Bob Lancaster's *Southern Strategy?* Tell me: Which of my choices leaves you sadly shaking your head? And what books have I overlooked?

Of course! How could I have forgotten that one?

Hoke, Miss Daisy, and Us

Driving Miss Daisy is the kind of movie that defeats glib judgments. That is, if you grew up in certain latitudes (the American South) at a certain time (the '40s and '50s) with certain ideas you never admitted to yourself or never explored fully—and couldn't explore fully if you had several lifetimes. It's the kind of movie you need to come to terms with.

Friends kept telling me I needed to see the movie. My son called to tell me to see it. And yet there was a peculiar reticence about the way they recommended it. It wasn't the way you would plug an Indiana Jones flick with a few hints about the chase scenes. They seemed to be saying: First see it, later we'll talk.

It was as if they didn't want to crowd me. It's the kind of movie you want to absorb alone, depending on where you've come from and where you're at now. Now, having seen the movie, I believe I understand the reticence. This is not a film you compare notes about afterward, or want to argue about. We saw it with some friends last week, and what we did over coffee afterward was mention the names of people the characters reminded us of—people we had known growing up. And then we pretty much stopped. The movie has an intimacy about it you don't want to violate.

Driving Miss Daisy is about the relationship between a Southern widow and her chauffeur, which is like saying *The Tempest* is a play about a father and his daughter. The widow, played exquisitely by Jessica Tandy, as she plays everything, is Southern, Jewish, and a lady. The chauffeur is black, aging himself, and—how shall I put it—a *mensch*. That's Yiddish for a real person, someone who tries to do the decent thing whatever his circumstances. Miss Daisy is the kind of nice Southern Reform Jewish lady who may not have much Yiddish, but knows what a *mensch* is. She is one. Eventually she comes to recognize one in Hoke, the chauffeur. He is played by Morgan Freeman with a sociological exactitude so perfect that it's natural. It's beyond science; it's art. It's as if every old black man who ever taught you anything were up there on the screen. And the screenplay, the *language,* is so right. I believe I heard only one unSouthern use of "y'all" in the singular.

There was an exception to all these recommendations for *Driving Miss Daisy.* Not a single black friend suggested I see the movie. One, a professor at the local branch of the university, thought the black character too submissive. She was clearly bothered by the praise heaped on the picture and on Morgan Freeman, who after all plays a servant. She didn't much care for Miss Daisy and her snooty ways, either.

Granted, the characters in the movie observed the outward forms of the caste system called Segregation—even as they rose above its essence. In the end they demonstrated a charity for one another that a 1990 audience may not be capable of. I don't mean my black friends are prepared to swallow Spike Lee's inept propaganda; my friends are smarter than that. But they're rightly suspicious of sentimentality about the informal relationships that held us together in the South when, formally and legally, we were supposed to be separate.

But those informal relationships did exist. And there was more than sentimentality to them. There was loyalty, friendship, humor, love...and other qualities not as admirable. Yes, we failed one another, as we often fail our friends. I remember a little sign my father used to keep above his desk: If We Want a Friend Without a Fault, We Shall Never Have a Friend.

In those days we were more able to forgive one another, and even ourselves. Now ideological tests seem to have taken the place of friendship. It is not a great advance. Now we tend to feel guilty or ashamed of people who could treat one another decently and normally in a system that was neither decent nor normal. We shouldn't be. We could show the past a little more charity. We could be a little more tolerant of others, and even of ourselves. Just as Miss Daisy and Hoke came to be.

One of the names that came to me after seeing *Driving Miss Daisy* was Henry's. Henry Johnson had worked for my father in Shreveport as long as I could remember, even before we had moved from above the store downtown out to Forrest Avenue. My father changed wares but never locations, and with each change Henry learned a new business (shoe repair, dry goods, pawnbroker, furniture) and in turn taught my father its finer points. Henry taught me how to work, and not to work for trash—that is, folks who don't care whether you do a good job or not, and who probably couldn't tell if you didn't. He also taught me all manner of manners, including how to ask for directions when we delivered furniture. You do *not* just whip into a gas station in front of the paying customers and yell out the window. You pull over to the side, get out, walk over to the attendant, exchange greetings, and then ask. Like a *mensch*. Henry Johnson died in 1980 a few weeks before my father did—as if he and Ben Greenberg would be inseparable in the next world, too.

It is a fallacy dating back to the ancient Greeks that friends must be equal in order to be friends. Servant and master are not equal, but to deny that they can be friends is to fly in the face of common experience, or at least mine. It is often inequality, and the capacity for bridging it, that gives friendship a special savor, and opens the door to justice.

But you don't want to listen to somebody else talk about *Driving Miss Daisy*. You don't want to see it from the outside in but from the inside out. You don't want to judge it but let it judge you, jostle your memory, and get you thinking.

Arkansan vs. Arkansawyer

Two Words, Two Worlds

In the summer of 1962, I realized that I would never be a very good graduate student or a very good anything else in New York City. The only part of my New York routine that I had relished was a chance to visit Washington, D. C. For a boy originally from Shreveport, arriving in Washington's old, pre-restored Union Station with its vaulted ceilings, muggy air, redcaps, and remnant of courtesy had been like going home.

And then to arrive in Pine Bluff that summer looking for a job was to experience a change in era as well as latitude. My first morning in Pine Bluff, I walked out of the old Pines Hotel, even then going to seed, into a cloudless southern morning, already glaring bright at nine.

"Can you tell me which way to the *Pine Bluff Commercial?*" I asked the first passerby. Dressed in khaki shirt and pants, he came to a complete stop. He nodded. He looked me in the eye. He seemed to have all the time in the world to talk with a stranger. He took me by the arm. He walked us over to the edge of the sidewalk so we could peer as far up Main as possible, toward the gold dome of the Jefferson County Courthouse. "It's past the railroad tracks," he said, motioning, "straight up the street about four blocks. On the left. About half a block before you get to the courthouse." I couldn't miss it. I was home.

It wasn't just the sun that warmed me as I made those four blocks. It was the pace. The air of civility. The sense of the fullness of time. The wave of gratitude for a small thing done well, even with a certain ceremony. The blend of familiarity *and* formality: the hand on the arm, the civil and obliging but not cringing tone. The understanding of what was important: human contact.

That day I would learn a new word at the elbow of the legendary Pat Owens, the paper's editorial page editor. He was looking for someone to spell him while he went off on a Nieman Fellowship, and I was looking for a job, a breather from graduate school, a living, maybe even a vocation. The word that kept showing up in copy was: Arkansan. I figured out what it meant almost immediately, and how to pronounce it after only a few exposures. Before that day, I hadn't thought much about what you call a resident of Arkansas. I might have guessed Arkansawan (wrong) or Arkansawyer (right).

It took me much longer to realize that Arkansan was also a kind of code word, a bellwether of everything bright, shiny, and better—a step toward the brave new world of civic uplift that would replace or at least subvert all those qualities I had luxuriated in earlier that morning. And for the next thirty years or so I would devote myself to spreading various subversive ideas—racial integration, economic development and diversification, higher educational standards— all of which would change the brave old world that greeted me so warmly that sunny day in '62. If there is a single word that sums up those new ideas and ways, it would not be Progress; we all know better than that now. No, the word would be Arkansan, a New South word if there ever was one.

As for the word that summed up the qualities of the past, it would be: Arkansawyer. It has a country sound about it, a rural informality, a certain contempt for what the world calls Progress. Which of course is why it fell into disuse, or was pushed. The man in khaki who showed me the way to the *Pine Bluff Commercial* was no Arkansan; he was an Arkansawyer. Where the state and maybe the South goes in the future may be determined by the tension between those two words and worlds: Arkansan and Arkansawyer.

By the 1970s, the concept of Arkansan already had triumphed over its rival. New and newer Souths had come and gone. Orval Faubus had given way to a succession of reform governors, and blue skies were shining above, nothing but blue skies from now on. So much has changed and so little has. The grasseaters have given way to white-collar segs, negrophobia to an attenuated snobbism, colorful pols to bland ones, and xenophobia is fading into imitativeness. The Eternal Incumbent is now Bill Clinton, the good ol' boys grow yuppified, and even the special interests have been slightly updated. Only the legislature, its old guard and oldthink still firmly in place, seems unchanged in spirit if not style.

Does the Man-in-Khaki yet live? You don't see much khaki anymore in this blue-jeaned age. Arkansawyers, as distinct from Arkansans, still abound, but they no longer are the norm. Pine Bluff has grown a mobile middle class, and you can no longer tell a stranger in town by the way he looks. For the moment there may be no cultural norm as Arkansan and Arkansawyer vie for dominance. There isn't much of an aristocracy left to manipulate and mediate between the two words and worlds; the old code has given way to a merchandising mentality that looks on Arkansas as another product to be pushed.

When the Arkansawyers go, what will happen to the qualities that greeted me, and showed me the way, that bright morning in the summer of '62? The innate courtesy. The good humor. The flow and traction of human contact. The conversation and the silences. The independence of spirit, if not means. The sense of personal honor that undergirds it all, and that could always be appealed to. When it was gone, at least it was obviously gone. Its absence or presence is no longer as clear today, perhaps because we are no longer as interested in it.

"The anguish that most of us have observed for some time now has been caused not by the fact that the South is alienated from the rest of the country, but by the fact that it is not alienated enough, that every day we are getting more and more like the rest of the country, that we are being forced out not only of our many sins, but of our few virtues."—Flannery O'Connor, of course.

By now the process Miss O'Connor noted has gone on long enough for the anguish to fade—like the pain in a nerve that is about dead. Only a tickle remains, and a memory we understand less and less.

The Arkansas of the Arkansawyers had to be one of the most contrary states in the Union: persnickety and accepting, divided and united, generous and stingy, warm-hearted and suspicious, short-sighted and dreamy, independent and partisan, hateful and lovable, honorable and despicable, maddening and delightful, hostile and hospitable...as divided as its topography. But from the Ozarks to the flatlands, that Arkansas was invariably proud, at least in style. If we ever succeed in straightening out all those qualities and reducing them to a mere consistency, there will be no Arkansas left. It will have become only a geographic, not an emotional, designation.

Besides pride, there is another consistent thread in the political, social, and psychological makeup of the species Arkie. (Arkie is another good word now informally banned by a combination of time, fashion, historical circumstance, and snobbism in general.) That quality is a consistent respect for integrity, though not as the world defines and limits it. No, the integrity Arkies respect and can even still halfway recognize is not mere honesty but a larger and related aggregation having to do with following one's own code.

The Arkansas idea of integrity may be impossible to spell out, but you know it when you see it. It shone in the band of women who got together to save Little Rock's public school system when the men couldn't. It showed up in the occasional gentleman—like Joe Hardin of Grady—who would run against Orval E. Faubus just because somebody should.

The most authentic Arkansas election return I ever saw was the list of winners in 1968: George Wallace for president, Winthrop Rockefeller for governor, J. William Fulbright for senator. That set of choices was pure Arkinsaw—in its inconsistency, its independence, and in its yearning for leaders who represent a faithfulness to some inner code. Even if they only *represented* integrity rather than embodied it. That set of returns would be inexplicable in almost any other state. One problem with keeping reform alive and appealing in Arkansas is that, once a nice bland form of it becomes the norm, it loses touch with the kind of eccentricity that, to the Arkansawyer, is the seal of integrity.

The challenge of saving the vanishing Arkansawyer is not unlike that faced by those who set out to save the Buffalo River in North Arkansas. To have left it alone, as some urged, would have left it open to all the commercial spoliations of modernity, brutal and subtle, from trash dumps to plastic-and-vinyl resorts. But to save it by wrapping the river in sacrosanct national parkland, like a shiny new product in a blister pack, was also to change its character.

As we compete with the rest of the Union and the rest of the world, which means to become more like it, it becomes harder to retain the essence of Arkansas, or maybe of the South—an essence that involves the refusal to compete at some things. Despite the standard Booster

Lit reference to Arkansas's work ethic, an advertisement with some basis in reality, what distinguishes Southerners is an ethic that will not let us define ourselves by our work. In Arkansas, this resistance to Americanization may be a by-product of what was once described as "the amazing and all but timeless Ozarkian talent for sustaining remoteness." That sense of remoteness amidst today's post-modernity allows the Arkansawyer to have a code of his own, rather than trade it in for this year's model from time to time. But as Arkansan succeeds Arkansawyer, and the state is Americanized, there emerges the competitive Arkansan, as advanced and jittery a specimen as any other striver. Have you noticed that "competitive" is now used as praise—as a consummation of our development devoutly to be wished? Once it would have been a dismissive description in what passed for polite society in these latitudes.

The tragedy is not so much that the Arkansan has lost contact with his past, but that increasingly he is either unaware or secretly proud that he has. And so he is rendered defenseless against anybody or any idea sufficiently removed from Arkansas to appear new, which is the standard American synonym for better. See how pliant the Arkansan becomes at the appearance of any outside consultant in clean fingernails and suitcoat. Then, when the newest nostrums fail, the inevitable reaction sets in. The resulting resentment lays down a rich soil for the demagogue, the standpatter, and all the champions of things as they once were and damned well should have stayed.

Reform is not an agenda, though it may have one. Reform is a spirit and, unless it can be personified, it will not move a stubborn and independent people. Once rendered impersonal and unappetizing, reform will either be frustrated by the old order or degenerate into a populism empty of any actual accomplishment.

The structural problems facing the South's politics and economy are not the greatest stumbling blocks to reform. They have been overcome before. The greatest problem is the difficulty of personalizing politics. What's missing is some central political figure, like a Faubus, who could symbolize all that is socially baneful, economically destructive, politically undemocratic, and morally offensive in The

System. What an inspiration, what a daily goad, he was to reformers.

Arkansans may be satisfied with a program; Arkansawyers need a personality, or at least a set of values to rally 'round or 'gainst. Arkansawyers are not much for abstract art; we crave the representational, the symbolic, the personal. It's an old and ingrained taste. Back in Jeff Davis's time, the editor of the *Pine Bluff Commercial* complained: "The trouble at the present day is that men and not principles are engaging the crowd.... The desire of the people to be amused instead of to be instructed inspires the motive of every political gathering. The standards of high discussion are misplaced by those of ribaldry, fustian, and rant." But it will not do to ignore the personal and the colorful, the rousing and symbolic; they must be appealed to, or against.

It is time for another great renewal, but it may not happen without a dominating figure or issue. The Arkansawyer in each of us demands some drama with his social, economic, and political uplift. Or he may accept only drama in place of it. Arkansas is still the land of the future, but unless someone can unite Arkansans and Arkansawyers behind a common vision, it always will be.

VI | THE NATION

The Big Scare

Once again America is a magnet for people all over the world. An estimated 600,000 legal immigrants manage to make it in every year plus who knows how many illegals. They obviously know something—namely, that this is still the land of opportunity, of freedom, of growth and yet stability. They are paying this society the greatest of compliments, and presenting it with the greatest of opportunities.

What other country has so many people banging on the gates wanting to work, invent, or think their way to the top? But that's not the way some Americans see immigration. They see something to fear, prevent, discourage. The xenophobia begins to grow thick.

You can sense it in the increasing number of states adopting English, or their version of it, as an official language—as if a language could be imposed by legal fiat. (Tell it to the Canadians, who started their language war some time ago and have reaped only division.) English, or rather American, already is the national language here. And if the past is any prologue, the American version of it will be enriched, not threatened, by these new waves of immigration.

To quote the third edition of H. L. Mencken's *The American Language,* published in 1923: "English now has the brakes on, but American continues to leap in the dark and the prodigality of its movement is all the indication that is needed of its intrinsic health, its capacity to meet the ever-changing needs of a restless and emotional people, constantly fluid in racial composition, and disdainful of tradition." May it ever be so.

Immigration and its discontents were already a familiar combination in Mr. Mencken's time. As the last century wound down, there was a new wave of immigration then, too—from Southern and Eastern Europe. The newcomers were flooding the great cities and inspiring the usual reaction: outcries and quotas. The accusations against them were numerous: They were ruining the economy, creating slums, turning America into a polyglot Babel, endangering democracy.... It's clearer now how baseless such fears were, and that the New Immigrants were essentially repeating the history of the old. They were really spurring the economy, moving out of the slums, enriching the language, and taking up democracy with the fervor of the newly converted.

But now, a century later, the newest New Immigration stirs the same fears, and produces the same hysterical reactions. The most xenophobic press release to arrive of late came from the Rockford Institute, which distributed an ugly little alarum written by Thomas J. Fleming, who is editor of its publication, *Chronicles*. Dr. Fleming has given up on the old argument that immigrants cost others jobs—now that study after study has shown that they take work no one else will, and contribute more to the American economy than they take. Instead, he warns that the influx of immigrants from non-European stock may wipe out American culture.

"The trouble begins," Dr. Fleming explains, "with treating the nation as an abstraction: the land of the free and the home of the brave was turned into the land of opportunity for what the Statue of Liberty's plaque so quaintly calls 'the wretched refuse' of the world. But the language and culture, as well as the legal and political systems, were derived from Britain. This way of life of ours is not the result of any general principle; it is the legacy of our forebears and a civilization that goes back to Greece and Rome. It is vastly creative and has shown an enormous capacity for transforming immigrants from somewhat differing cultures. This capacity is not infinite."

The trouble with Dr. Fleming's thesis begins with treating the nation as a product of genetics or geography rather than of ideas that know no ethnic boundaries. And of course America is an abstraction: Our fathers brought forth on this continent a new nation, conceived in liberty, and dedicated to the proposition that all men are created equal. If Mr. Lincoln was right about that, and he was, what could be a more abstract basis for nationhood?

Emma Lazarus's words on the Statue of Liberty are anything but quaint; they are still relevant, alive, moving: "Give me your tired, your poor / Your huddled masses yearning to breathe free / The wretched refuse of your teeming shore..."

One would not want to disappoint Dr. Fleming, but the national motto is not *E Pluribus Britannica*. If the American language and culture, as well as legal and political systems, were derived from Britain, where do you suppose jazz, Faulkner, tacos and the Frontier Spirit came from? Not to mention judicial review (the most distinctive feature of the American constitutional system) and the idea of a written constitution itself. Notions that never gained sway in Britain, like the separation of church and state, have become the norm here.

To quote D. W. Brogan, an Englishman of greater percipience than many an American scholar, "The study of American political organization and method imposes on the European student a humility before the facts that may not come easily. Even if his admiration for the British Constitution is as warm and uncritical as that of Burke, Macaulay or Woodrow Wilson, he must remember that he is inspecting a system based on different principles and formed by a different experience.... He must be willing to notice the extraordinary phenomena he is studying, without reacting like the farmer who saw the giraffe and said, 'impossible.'"

America is not a New Europe but, as the dollar bill says, *Novus Ordo Seclorum,* a New Order of the Ages. Its roots go back beyond Greece and Rome—to ancient Israel, if not farther, yet this society has always faced forward, toward the future. America's capacity for absorbing new and ever newer migrations may not be infinite, as John Fleming notes, but it is far greater than his frightened little estimate.

Dr. Fleming speaks of America transforming the immigrant but seems unaware of how much the immigrant has transformed America and made it more...American. He underestimates the transforming power of the land itself, and of our experience on it.

Recommended reading: Robert Frost's "The Gift Outright." ("The land was ours before we were the land's...") Or Daniel Boorstin's *The Genius of American Politics*—and particularly its theory of givenness, "the belief that values in America are in some way automatically defined: *given* by certain facts of geography or history peculiar to us." America is not European culture, let alone British culture, simply transported to a blank canvas.

Thomas Fleming also pays his respects to our neighbors to the South: "It was the barbarians that brought the Roman Empire down, and we shall be in even worse straits if we fail to control our Southern border." History can be trusted to judge who acted like barbarians in Mexico and other parts of this New World: the indigenous peoples or the representatives of European "civilization" who conquered, massacred and enslaved them.

The way out for America lies in reviving the immigration laws of the 1920s, according to Dr. Fleming. Those laws, he said, "made it very clear that we intended to be what we had always been: a European nation." Preferably a Western European nation, since that's the way the quotas were skewed. If those laws hadn't been changed, the late Leopold Tyrmand—a scholar who ornamented the Rockford Institute when it was turning out invariably respectable work, a writer of charm, humility and insight who devoted himself to defending America to the Americans—might have had a much harder time getting into this country from his native Poland.

A Certain Slant of Light

There's a certain slant of light,
On winter afternoons,
That oppresses, like the weight
Of cathedral tunes.

November 22. In the middle of the car wreck or the plunge down the mountainside or in the mind of the drowning, time slows, then stops—the way it does for some Americans every year when the page of the calendar is torn away and today's date revealed: November 22.

It is always 12:29 Dallas time when the motorcade comes into sight. Emily Dickinson's certain slant of light is recorded on celluloid now in the form of the Zapruder film. Click: The presidential limousine coming down Houston makes a sharp left onto Elm. Click: The President is smiling, waving. Click: Mrs. Kennedy looks at him with concern. Click: A bystander jerks his head suddenly toward Dealey Plaza. Click: The limousine is lost behind a street sign. Click: The President reaches for his throat, slumps toward his wife. Click: The governor of Texas, seated in front of the President, falls forward. Click: The shattering impact. Click: Mrs. Kennedy rises. Click: She is pushed back into the car by a Secret Service agent. Click: The limousine disappears from view beneath the underpass, heading for Parkland Hospital and history. The film runs 15 seconds. And an eternity.

To watch the Zapruder film is to see the destruction of the temple again and again. Mortality casts its shadow over not only a President but a Republic. Young America would never be quite so young again. After that, nothing was the same. Events seemed to spin out of control. Click: The anguish of Vietnam. Click: Martin Luther King Jr. on the balcony of the Lorraine Motel at Memphis. Click: Robert Kennedy, after his victory speech, in a pool of blood. Click: A President announcing he would not risk election. Click: A President disgraced. Click: A President unable to cope.

Looking back, it all seemed to start at 12:29, Dallas time, November 22, 1963, and it would take years, decades to rebuild American confidence. Nor is the work complete. One generation of Americans may never be quite so sure—of anything—again. It was a harrowing way to come of age.

The representatives of 220 nations were there to follow the seven matched grays pulling the caisson and casket, followed by the restless, riderless horse. De Gaulle was there, and Haile Selassie. The Cabinet was there, and the Joint Chiefs of Staff—the representatives of the whole panoply of earthly powers that could not save the young President.

"There is an appointed time for everything," the priest intoned at the state funeral, "a time to be born and a time to die...a time to love and a time to hate...a time of war and a time of peace..." A time to build up and a time to tear down, and November 22, 1963, marked the beginning of a great tearing down. Never again, I thought at the time, would Americans take their leaders so lightly, their institutions so surely.

Americans suddenly, grievously learned to cherish old values anew: continuity and stability, moderation and order, duration and legality. In a country and culture synonymous with change, we had almost forgotten how important those values are, and how American. Not just the vulnerability of a President but of the presidency had been driven home.

But time passes and fortune smiles, and the most blessed of nations finds it easy to forget, and falls into complacency. Hubris is the child of forgetfulness. Then some new crisis erupts, and the people are reminded again of how important and how demanding are the institutions of the Republic—of any republic. The instruments of democracy are not machines that run themselves, no matter how wondrous or complicated they may seem, or be. Sometimes, as on November 22nd, it doesn't take a crisis to remind the nation of the fragility of life and power, just a date on the calendar and a certain slant of light—

When it comes, the landscape listens,
Shadows hold their breath;
When it goes, 'tis like the distance
On the look of death.

The Death of the Symbolic

By the same 5-to-4 margin by which it overruled a Texas law protecting the flag, the Supreme Court of the United States now has overturned a federal statute that was a transparent attempt to get around its earlier ruling. That figures. Once the court decided that Americans have a constitutional right to burn their flag, no mere statute could protect it. From the outset, the Bush Administration was less than enthusiastic about a flag law, anticipating just this result. It was right.

Now let's do what should have been done directly after the Supreme Court's first ruling: Correct it by a simple, limited constitutional amendment. It should take no more than a couple of dozen words to make it clear that nothing in this Constitution shall prevent the states or the federal government from outlawing the physical desecration of the flag of the United States. Period. No fuss, no muss, no wispy federal statutes. No mischievous language that might hinder freedom of speech or prevent depictions of the flag. No gratuitous clauses that might keep a cop, soldier or teenager from wearing a flag patch as part of the uniform of the day.

What the court has done by the narrowest of majorities is to confuse action with speech. Burning the flag, it has decided, is symbolic speech. Why not punching out one's neighbor, or blowing up the Supreme Court chambers? Surely such actions are not protected by the First Amendment, any more than mutilating the flag of the United States should be. Just because an action expresses an idea (many actions do) doesn't mean it should be lawful.

Justice William J. Brennan liked his opinion in the original flag-burning case so much that he quoted it again: "If there is a bedrock principle underlying the First Amendment, it is that the Government may not prohibit the expression of an idea simply because society finds the idea itself offensive or disagreeable."

But it isn't the idea itself that society found offensive in the flag-burning case. This defendant could have stood on a street corner all day long and badmouthed the flag of the United States—and motherhood and apple pie, too—and nobody would have much cared. It's a free country. It was burning Old Glory—an action—that brought the law down on him, at least till the Supreme Court called it symbolic speech.

The bedrock principle on which Mr. Justice Brennan takes his stand is more like a pool of quicksand. If our protester in Texas had killed somebody as an expression of his complete and unexpurgated freedom of symbolic speech, would Justice Brennan finally have discerned the line between legal speech and illegal action? Let's hope so, but there's no telling for sure from his jurisprudence.

Is it because "only" a flag, a symbol, was destroyed that action became speech? "We live by symbols," Felix Frankfurter noted in another and more eloquent decision of the Supreme Court half a century ago. A society that does not guard its symbols is on its way to becoming something other than a society: an atomized herd, maybe. If we live by symbols, we also die with them. Another civilization once decided that its symbolic protest would be to burn books, and it became an anti-civilization. If the law is a great teacher, it can teach barbarism as well as civilization. What message has the Supreme Court sent by these decisions? That it is permissible to burn the flag of the United States. Now it is time for The People to send a better one.

The message, simple and clear and dispassionate, should be that it is a crime to burn the flag of the United States. It is a crime in a larger sense than the violation of a statute. It is offensive—an offense against what binds all of us together. "The ultimate foundation of a free society," Felix Frankfurter wrote in that 1940 decision, "is the binding tie of cohesive sentiment." That is what the flag symbolizes, and flags are not for burning—any more than tombstones are for toppling or churches for vandalizing. We have laws against such things not solely or even principally because tombstones or churches are a form of property, though they are, but because they represent something beyond their material value. They transcend their physical form—just as the flag does. But alas, if there is one thing that modern, tolerant society will not tolerate it is the transcendent.

Call it the Death of the Symbolic. Or maybe the Reverence Deficit. The American flag represents a bond to be revered. Perhaps that is why we call its mutilation a desecration. The literary critic George Steiner notes that ever since the dawn of the modern age, societies have been borrowing symbolic language "from the bank or treasure-house of theology" and the result is that we have "made small change of the reserves of transcendent authority." Until finally it has become impossible for five out of nine justices of the Supreme Court to view a physical attack on the symbol of the nation as a punishable offense.

Symbols are now demystified until they become only raw materials for the "science" of semiotics—just as literature is "deconstructed." It is all part of a strange modern version of freedom that has become indistinguishable from emptiness. When we permit Old Glory to be burned in protest, Brother Brennan explains, it shows how much we respect that for which it stands. By letting it be destroyed, we honor it. Uh huh. If a fellow didn't know this was law, he might strongly suspect it was nonsense.

Enough. Let us return to meaning, which often has to do with the correct reading of symbols and a proper respect for them. Let us return to law and its enforcement. One no-nonsense constitutional amendment to go, please. Let's make one payment on the immense debt we owe to the "merely" symbolic. Long may she wave.

Whither Civil Rights?

This year, to celebrate the birthday of Martin Luther King Jr., there was a march on the campus of the University of Arkansas at Pine Bluff. The songs were still the same, and the speeches hadn't changed much, either. It should have been like old times. It wasn't.

For one thing, it would have been hard to imagine a civil rights march on this campus back in the early Sixties when it was still all-black Arkansas AM&N. One of the principal chores of its chancellor then was to keep the lid on—an assignment he performed adeptly. For another, there was none of the old sense of urgency, or danger. This wasn't history so much as an historical pageant. The form had been preserved; the spirit had to be imagined.

For those impelled to continue The Struggle, it's something of a sacrilege to say it's been won. But it has. The essentially formal, political, legal goals of those days were achieved—in schools, in the voting booth, even at the lunch counter. That is why the spirit of those days is no longer recapturable.

Yes, there are still gaps to fill in the law, particularly in its enforcement. But anyone who can remember the freedom riders and sit-ins of the 1960s has lived through one of the most successful and relatively peaceful revolutions of this century. It is difficult to think of any other caste system in the world that has been overthrown, at least outwardly, with such dispatch, law and order. Nor is it easy to imagine any sentient Southerner who would willingly return to the era of segregated schools and poll taxes.

The challenge now is less political or legal than economic and social. To continue to fight the same old battles against the same old enemies (Racism! Discrimination!) by using the same old tactics is to reduce the cause of civil rights to an historical pageant—and to ignore today's different and more dangerous foe.

If there still were a civil rights movement instead of a civil rights establishment, perhaps Ronald Reagan would have inspired a more thoughtful response when, in a parting shot, he noted that some black spokesmen "are doing very well leading organizations based on keeping alive the feeling that they're victims of prejudice." Immediately the air was full of defensive reactions. Anybody who thought Mr. Reagan might be on to something knew better than to speak out and violate the same taboo he had. And so the usual Bonfire of the Vanities proceeded uninterrupted—until it died out shortly from lack of interest. When no one dares discuss real concerns, real dialogue is impossible.

Why not say it? There is no longer a civil rights movement, at least not in the sense of the 1960s. Mainly because those rights have been largely secured. Instead, there is a stultified roster of civil rights organizations, or campy burlesques of civil rights struggles like the Tawana Brawley Affair in New York starring Big Al Sharpton and his little sharpies. Have you noticed that the very term Civil Rights has acquired the same suspect patina that some time ago did in another once respectable term, Welfare? Words are the currency of thought, and can be abused only so long before losing their original value.

The great unmentionable in discussions of civil rights today is the mundane observation that racial discrimination is no longer the basis of the most serious problems that beset black Americans. Racism may make a great scapegoat but it is not a cogent explanation for the social pathology raging in black ghettoes. No racist could do what drugs, crime, ignorance and family disorganization have done there.

Let's remember that Black America has become a two-tiered community, and that where education, family, the work ethic and the black church have played their part, black Americans are thriving. Compared with the 1960s, there are now twice as many black families making more than $50,000 a year. It's estimated that the black middle class has grown by a third in the 1980s—from 3.6 million to 4.8 million—and is now larger than either the black working class or the black poor. This statistical portrait is scarcely a reflection of pervasive racism.

It's the horrendous figures for the black underclass that disturb: Since the 1960s, the number of black families making under $5,000 a year has increased almost a third—at a time of general economic expansion. The percentage of young black males who dropped out of the labor market between 1982 and 1987—five boom years—actually *increased* from 21 to 22 percent.

There are far more dangerous villains preying on black Americans than racial discrimination, notable among them the breakdown of the black family and the depredations of a welfare system that might better be called illfare. The system's effects have been ruinous and even now it is not being reformed but only slightly disguised.

To quote Walter Williams, professor of economics and font of candor: "I know of no one who would treat their children as we treat poor people. They would not provide incentives for their 14-year-old daughters to have babies. They stress to their children the importance of education. They often see to it that their children live with the unpleasant consequences of their behavior. Do they show the same compassion and common sense toward the poor? No, they take the position that the poor have a right to dependency."

What could induce dependency more surely than blaming all one's ills on invincible, ineradicable prejudice? Even after the political goals of the civil rights movement have been largely achieved, the economic and social challenge remains as formidable as ever, and it requires an economic and social response, not another re-enactment of the same old political drama.

The vision of the old civil rights movement is now largely a reality. The political approach advocated earlier this century by W.E.B. DuBois has been largely achieved. The most neglected and sometimes even despised figure in the black pantheon remains Booker T. Washington, who understood that political power without economic self-sufficiency, without a solid economic and social base, would prove a cruel and fleeting drama. And that is just what is happening to the half of Black America that is being left behind.

Now is the time to revive Booker T. Washington's old lessons, dull and apolitical and businesslike as they may seem. "Cast down your bucket where you are," he advised. It will no longer do to look to the system for emancipation; the system has done pretty much what it can for the poor and, where welfare is concerned, to the poor. This is a time for *auto*-emancipation.

The New Segism

Robert L. Williams, a psychology professor at Washington University, says black Americans should be given separate aptitude tests because the ones currently used are biased in favor of Americans of European stock. This will strike a familiar chord among those of us who remember when blacks were given not just separate tests but entirely separate educations. That system was called segregation; it was supposed to be separate but equal, just as Robert Williams's tests doubtless would be.

Dr. Williams himself seems to have mastered all-American psychobabble, to judge by his argument for separate-but-equal testing: "Black lifestyles should be examined and understood in terms of their historical, cultural and social realities and not in terms of a comparison with the experiences of other groups, for example Euro-Americans." Anybody who can drop the word Lifestyles into the conversation should be able to pronounce Euro-Americans without even swallowing hard.

How long would it be, one wonders, before those designing these new separate-but-equal tests would have to work out the kind of cockeyed racial categories that bedeviled practitioners of other forms of racial segregation? Would mulattoes take the test for whites or the one for blacks? Or half of each? Would middle-class blacks from Vermont who wouldn't know June Teen from July the Fourth get their pick of tests? Would all Southerners whose Lifestyles include day-long Sunday services, chitlins, and watermelon take the black test instead of having to wrestle with questions about how to drive on ice and snow?

Thirty years after Brown v. Board of Education, it's not that easy to find expert guidance on such serious matters; perhaps the rapidly fading authorities in South Africa could be called on for advice. They may be the only ones left with long experience in making such arcane distinctions.

If Dr. Williams's separate-but-equal tests became the vogue, there is no end to the groups, subgroups, in-groups, out-groups, offshoots and admixtures thereof that might qualify. "I have yet to see any problem, however complicated," Poul Anderson once opined, "which, when you looked at it the right way, did not become still more complicated." Dr. Williams has demonstrated that the same result may be achieved by looking at a problem the wrong way.

If biases can be found in this country's testing industry, and they can, then the proper response is to eliminate them, not multiply them for each hyphenated group of Americans. That way lies chaos. And it's been tried before—with unhappy results. Are we trying to build a society, or a Tower of Babel?

Dr. Williams is only one of the many well-intentioned contributors to what can only be called The New Segregationism. It manifests itself in a variety of ways great and small. The most evident may be quotas for blacks or Hispanics or some other official minority. (All Americans belong to one minority or another, but only some are officially recognized.) When an idea is corrupt, the language in which it is expressed must be corrupted first in order to make it acceptable. That's how "minorities" becomes a loose euphemism for blacks, as if "black" were a bad word.

Then there are the educators who insist that segregated schools still have a useful role to play in American life, at least when those schools are black. No seg ever defended predominantly white schools more effectively than predominantly black colleges are defended today. Ralph Bunche's old warning would surely be denounced as racist on many a black campus now: "We cannot prepare people to function in an integrated society by educating them in segregated institutions."

The New Segregationism, it is explained, is practiced *on behalf* of the minority, not against it, and that is what distinguishes it from the old, and justifies things like separate but equal testing. But many an old-fashioned seg thought of himself as a benefactor of the Negro when he argued for the separation of the races. Negroes, it was explained, were simply not equipped to make it in the larger culture, and those wild-eyed liberals who expected the Negro to compete on the same level as others were being unrealistic. It was simply unfair to expect Ralph Bunche, say, to measure up intellectually to the average member of the Ku Klux Klan.

The more rational of the old segregationists, aware of the imbecilities of such an argument, would carefully distinguish themselves from the white supremacists, explaining that they didn't believe Negroes were inferior but only different—historically, culturally, socially—and so must be judged by different standards. Dr. Williams strikes an eerily familiar note when he explains: "Black lifestyles should be examined and understood in terms of their historical, cultural and social realities and not in comparison with the experiences of other groups..." I've heard that one before. I grew up in the South hearing that one from cultivated segs.

The historical, social, and cultural reality that is ignored by segs old and new, conscious and unconscious, is that blacks are part of the larger culture, too. If blacks in this country must be called Afro-Americans, it is important to remember which is the adjective and which the noun.

Of course it is possible to segregate blacks—by tests and other devices. But to treat black Americans as a different species, for whatever malign or benign purpose, is to commit the same old mistake and to court the same sad results. Couldn't we just try integration—the real thing—before declaring it a failure? The new segism isn't likely to be any more wholesome than the old.

The Omelas Syndrome

It must be obvious that intellectual freedom in this country is most threatened on campus, and most threatened there by the Left. By now even the good, gray and slightly myopic *New York Times* seems to have noticed. ("At Stanford, Leftists Become Censors.")

One prestigious American university after another considers adopting a gag rule—though all make certain to call it a Speech Code. (Euphemism is the first sign of a deed one is ashamed of.) Schools where conventional values have been ridiculed for years now find themselves so shocked at attacks on their own unconventional ones that they resort to censorship by some milder name. The polite rationalizations offered for censorship on campus always remind me of a line from Ring Lardner: "'Shut up,' he explained." It would all be amusing if it weren't so pathetic—and dangerous. For censorship is surely most ominous in centers of learning.

Too late, various spokesmen for freedom try to explain why it's wrong to gag those one disagrees with, even when what they say is offensive or rude or disgusting. Charles Evans Hughes and Oliver Wendell Holmes are much quoted. Various truisms are repeated ("The best remedy for offensive speech is more, not less, speech.") The obvious is painfully repeated: "When you pass a rule which represses speech, you are avoiding dealing with the underlying problem and you're passing a rule whose sweep is going to be broader than the things you're trying to contain."

All this time-tested counsel seems to have little effect. One faculty after another is provoked by some incident or insult on campus into abridging its students' freedom. Places like Yale and Dartmouth set the pattern some time ago by trying to punish students who would not toe the acceptable ideological line; now Stanford has taken the lead. That figures. A school that would whittle down its readings in Western Culture is not likely to be troubled by sacrificing one of that culture's essentials: freedom of speech.

Perhaps the most revealing defense of suppression on campus came from Canetta Ivy, a member of the Council of Student Presidents at Stanford. Debating an imposition on free speech, she said, "What we are proposing is not completely in line with the First Amendment." But, she acknowledged, "I'm not sure it should be. We at Stanford are trying to set a standard different from what society at large is trying to accomplish."

Perhaps that's why all the lectures about freedom of speech aren't working; freedom is for the rest of us, not for a place with different and presumably higher standards—a kind of ideal society. Once again utopianism proves the richest soil for repression. Plato's *Republic* didn't put much store by freedom of speech, either. Maybe that's why citing arguments from Milton or Jefferson isn't very effective: those gentlemen were concerned with a real society—not a perfect, protected enclave.

What we have here is the Omelas Syndrome—named for the mythical city of "Omelas, bright-towered by the sea." It is more fully described in a jewel of a short story, "The Ones Who Walk Away From Omelas." In Omelas, life is perfect joy as imagined by each individual reader: religion without clergy, courage without soldiers, art without labor, triumph without any defeated. The only sacrifice asked in return is one small inconvenience that all must agree to tolerate:

"In a basement under one of the beautiful public buildings of Omelas, or perhaps in the cellar of one of its spacious private homes, there is a room. It has one locked door, and no window..." and in this foul place, which is described as intensely as the beauties of Omelas, there is a neglected, abandoned, feeble-minded, starved child whom all must agree to leave so. "Those are the terms." Indeed, they may be the only terms on which Utopia is possible: perfection in exchange for repression.

Some will not accept those terms, and leave. "They keep walking, and walk straight out of the city of Omelas, through the beautiful gates," says the writer of the story, "...they walk ahead into the darkness, and they do not come back. The place they go towards is a place even less imaginable to most of us than the city of happiness. I cannot describe it at all. It is possible that it does not exist. But they seem to know where they are going, the ones who walk away from Omelas."

The story can be read many ways but one way is to ask whether one would accept such perfection at the cost of just one little, abandoned, neglected, abused freedom: freedom of speech, with all its potential for pain, disagreement, uncertainty and offense. In the end the question being decided at university after university is: Should we walk away from Omelas?

Literature might make the choice clearer. Recommended reading: "The Ones Who Walk Away From Omelas," by Ursula K. Le Guin.

The Decline and Fall of Literacy

September is National Literacy Month, and there has been much ado about it. There should be. It's important to bring non-readers into the wider world. But being literate also means, or used to mean, something more than a capacity to read and write on an eighth-grade level. To say that someone is literate once implied a passing familiarity with literature, philosophy, a few of the arts and perhaps even some of the sciences. One definition of literate is still "an educated person," though that meaning is rapidly passing out of vogue. Alas, it's being replaced by oxymorons like Computer Literacy. Surely what is meant by Computer Literacy is competence at manipulating a computer, since being able to "think" like a machine would seem the opposite of literacy, which has something to do with thinking in words.

The older and broader definition of literacy needs reviving, if that is possible in an age that may be shaped more by television, word processors and spectator sports than by books. Illiteracy in the higher sense is not confined to those who can't read. "The man who does not read good books," Mark Twain once observed, "has no advantage over the man who can't read them."

Again and again, when people in this part of the country explain why they want to read, they mention the Bible. Raised on the spoken word, and long sustained by it, they are hungry for the written. Yet those who do read may pass by the family Bible—with its thunderous call, its joy and sorrows, its majesty and gentleness—on their way to turn on the television set. Shakespeare becomes something you had to study in school but outgrew in favor of the soaps. A larger proportion of Americans comes to depend on pictures and a trendy overlay of the spoken word to get the news and reach political judgments. Frightening.

Not that the Bible remains untouched. Sometimes hands are laid upon it, forcibly. The chief virtue of some newer translations is that they are sidesplittingly funny. That's the effect of turning the Elizabethan of the King James Version into modtalk. In his classic essay, "Politics and the English Language," George Orwell translated a once familiar biblical passage into modern English. See if you can identify it through his newspeak:

"Objective consideration of contemporary phenomena compels the conclusion that success or failure in competitive activities exhibits no tendency to be commensurate with innate capacity, but that a considerable element of the unpredictable must invariably be taken into account."

Give up? Here's the older, clearer version:

"I returned and saw under the sun, that the race is not to the swift, nor the battle to the strong, neither yet bread to the wise, nor yet riches to men of understanding, nor yet favour to men of skill; but time and chance happeneth to them all."

Ain't it the truth?

And in the King James, that truth is discernible. George Orwell wrote his essay more than 40 years ago, and language does not seem to have improved since. The kind of writing he described then may only have grown, like kudzu, till the meanings it covers are barely recognizable. His excruciating translation of the familiar verse from Ecclesiastes sounds like a typical passage from any modern text on education. History texts, which may have the most exciting stories to tell, have started to sound like sociology. The poetry has been drained, the meaning obscured, the simple made pretentious, and any interest on the reader's part converted instantly into utter boredom.

George Orwell set out to describe modern writing at its worst in the 1940s, and succeeded in capturing the spirit of ordinary prose in the 1980s: "As I have tried to show, modern writing at its worst does not consist in picking out words for the sake of their meaning and inventing images in order to make the meaning clearer. It consists in gumming together long strips of words which have already been set in order by someone else, and making the results presentable by sheer humbug." Sounds like he's describing a presidential campaign speech.

A voluntary illiteracy seems to have swept the country. Else, how explain some of the strange things said in public discourse, and the ready audience for solemn idiocies? Some days it seems Americans have tired of communicating and would rather just watch, or growl inarticulately. Not just the politicians but the voters mutter the same old tired but comforting shibboleths; it's easier than thinking. See the plodding pace of current campaigns. Words need not have much connection with thought to be strung together passably by today's standards. That much is abundantly illustrated by legal briefs, daily journalese, and Educanto, the species of non-language that has taken the place of English in academic circles.

A day in honor of literacy should concentrate not just on those who can't read but on those who won't. It's a time to praise, emulate, and preserve that endangered species—the critical reader. Let's proclaim reading and writing participation sports. And let's encourage those who look to the written word not only for convenience and advancement but for instruction, inspiration, provocation, and mystery.

I Love a Parade

Saturday's parade down Main Street got me thinking—about the troops returning from the Gulf, about parades, about the spirit of the time, and about the spirit of other times.

My father was one of those merchants who put their children in their advertisements. It couldn't have been because I was cute. Maybe it was a way of personalizing the various businesses he went through all at the same modest location on Texas Avenue in Shreveport: second-hand shoes and shoe repair, dry goods, furniture on easy credit terms...Ben Greenberg was a man of successive enthusiasms.

One reason I can remember them all is that the succession of calendars and flyers with my picture on them now represents a kind of photographic-commercial-cultural record of my childhood. I started out as The Little Shoemaker, age 3. Chubby with long locks, complete with shoemaker's apron, last, awl and hammer, there I am squinting into the Louisiana sun in 1940. (I still love the smell of leather and shoe repair shops. Doesn't everybody? The dust makes me both wheezy and nostalgic.)

Then came The War, Second World. The calendar for 1944, now on the back of my office door, shows a little boy in Army uniform—Class A, complete with brass buttons, tie, and garrison cap—almost lost midway to the summit of an immense mound of used Army boots in the warehouse my father had rented. He had become "Greenberg Shoe Company—Wholesale Dealer in Second Hand Shoes, Clothing & Hats." The message on the calendar proclaims: "For More Profit Buy Your Needs From The Little Shoemaker in the Army." I had been conscripted.

The picture says a lot about 1944: It was okay to depict little kids in uniform. The whole country was at war. Our house, I remember, was full of soldiers from the Army Air Force base at Barksdale. (There was an eligible daughter at home, and she wound up marrying one of them in a ceremony in which groom and best man wore their uniforms.) I can still remember almost all their first names, rank, and military specialties—bombardier, navigator, pilot, gunner, quartermaster, clerk-typist . . . .

Today they would be called role models. I went to movies at the base when the more tolerant boyfriends would let me tag along. Kids grew up knowing the difference between a P-47 Thunderbolt, P-51 Mustang, P-38 Lightning, and B-17 and B-24 bombers. We learned the outlines of enemy and allied planes from those little aircraft recognition cards that kids traded.

One knew without being told what the progression of life was: school, college, the service, a job or maybe graduate school before settling down. . . . The Service was as expected a stage as any other. One day I was buying comic books on Texas Street and the next marching down it with an M-1 on my shoulder in high school ROTC. It was only natural. One grew up seeing others in uniform—the role models—and then it was your turn. It was expected.

Then came a time—then came decades—when military service was viewed as something else. Not just something all the guys did but an aberration. Not just a necessary bother and maybe danger but an unfair exception to the natural scheme of things. An imposition. An unfair interruption. Why, it was almost un-American.

A different set of expectations took shape some time between Korea and Vietnam: The world was now supposed to be a nice, peaceful, secure place where wars were unnecessary and anybody stupid enough or unlucky enough to serve in the military certainly wasn't going to be considered a role model. Servicemen came back in the middle of the night one by one; parades went out of fashion.

Maybe it was stalemate and defeat that did it, or the general uncertainty about what was now expected of an enlightened citizen. Whatever the reason, to dress a seven-year-old in a military uniform—and then advertise it!—would have raised eyebrows.

The parade in Pine Bluff Saturday, like those all over the country, was more than a welcome home for the troops. It isn't just the troops who are returning but America itself—not just to duty but to certain realities:

There is no security without sacrifice.

There is no freedom without courage.

There is nothing shameful in victory.

There is such a thing as a just cause.

The message of Saturday's parade, and of all the homecomings that have greeted the returning troops, is simple. And it has gone too long unsaid to veterans of one conflict after another: You did a great job. We're proud of you. You remind us that the United States of America is a force for good in the world and that evil must be faced down. The uniform you wear is something to inspire pride and respect. Thank you. We had almost forgotten. And there are some things a free country cannot afford to forget.

Just Warming Up—After 214 Years

Everybody must have his own favorite part of a symphony concert— the tantalizing overture, the clashing finale, the emergence of the grand theme, the point and counterpoint. I confess to a weakness for that magical moment of anticipation before the concert proper, when the musicians drift onstage, each with instrument great or small, and begin the process of tuning up. The great hall slowly comes to life with the discordant sound of promise as each musician strives for the right key or burnishes a phrase. It is a moment alive with promise and anticipation. The future is warming up.

Two hundred and fourteen years after declaring its independence from the Old World and the old ways, the great American symphony is still being assembled. The instruments are still being sounded experimentally, the orchestra still gathering. Yet the whole world seems to be listening and trying to hum along.

In country after unexpected country, America has become the model, the rage, the light. And in those dark places that have not yet yielded to the freedom tide—in Castro's Cuba and China's gerontocracy—America remains the alternative, the subversive threat to tyranny it has been for 214 years. In Beijing's Tiananmen Square, the students paraded a Goddess of Democracy that bore a striking resemblance to the American Statue of Liberty. And though they would be crushed to earth, their spirit still lives, and will rise again. China's leaders sense it, and shudder. *Sic semper tyrannis*—so long as there is an America to emulate.

At a time when the word Revolution has lost its luster around the globe, so many crimes having been committed in its name, the product of the American Revolution remains the world's hope.

Last year, our town's 150th anniversary was celebrated in connection with Independence Day and, as part of the typically assorted program that marks such homespun festivities, I was asked to give a patriotic reading at the courthouse. In few other countries does oratory play so central a role in the national culture. Lacking the panoply of a royal court, the ritual of a national church, or even a national costume, Americans take succor in a national rhetoric.

What sample of American oratory would you have chosen to present? Surely no celebration of July the Fourth would be complete without a reading of The Great Declaration itself, with its assertion not only of American freedom but of freedom itself: We hold these truths to be self-evident, that all men are created equal, that they are endowed by their Creator with certain unalienable Rights, that among these are Life, Liberty, and the pursuit of Happiness.

The words still thrill, and not just Americans. Sweeping and bold, they pronounced the future, and still do. They ennoble but they also irritate. How inconvenient the words are for those who would like to be just a little more equal than others. And how those made uncomfortable at such words have tried to explain away their clear meaning over the years. But they cannot. Mr. Jefferson's prose still rings, not only in celebration but in promise, and in accusation against every form of tyranny—abroad and in ourselves.

Abe Lincoln understood. On his way to assume the presidency of a sundered Union and somehow bind it together, Mr. Lincoln paused to visit Independence Hall, where the Great Declaration was first read. And he reminded the nation that there is "something in that Declaration giving liberty, not alone to the people of this country, but hope to the world for all future time. It was that which gave promise that in due time the weights should be lifted from the shoulders of all men, and that all should have an equal chance. This is the sentiment embodied in that Declaration of Independence."

It still is.

And when the shining words are pronounced again, the mystic chord of memory struck and the promise renewed, let us not ignore the dark underside of the Declaration, the jangle and off-key notes, the counterpoint of certain realities. Let us read the words of Frederick Douglass on the Fourth of July, 1852, spoken in the shadow of the Fugitive Slave Act:

"What to the American slave is your Fourth of July? I answer: a day that reveals to him, more than all other days of the year, the gross injustice and cruelty to which he is the constant victim.... You invite to your shores fugitives of oppression from abroad, honor them with banquets, greet them with ovations, cheer them, toast them, salute them, protect them, and pour out your money to them... but the fugitive from your own land you advertise, hunt, arrest, shoot and kill. You glory in your refinement and your universal education; yet you maintain a system as barbarous and dreadful as ever stained the character of a nation—a system begun in avarice, supported in pride, and perpetuated in cruelty."

What is the test of American oratory? That it hides nothing. Not the fate of the red man, or the compromises with expedience, or the poverty, ignorance and vice that still stalk the land. Candor, too, is part of the greatness of America. It may explain the American capacity for change, and why it remains the land of the future.

Henry David Thoreau, no mean rhetorician himself, claimed that Americans "love eloquence for its own sake, and not for any truth which it may utter, or any heroism it may inspire..." That is an overstatement typical of American oratory. As much as we love the sheer sound of the words themselves (what more beautiful words than

Republic? Independence? Endowed by Their Creator?) those words also reflect certain values. Those values will need to be tuned and renewed as this experiment, this concert of ideas, this grand amalgamation and fulfillment, gathers and proceeds.

At the courthouse last year, I chose to give Patrick Henry's speech on the ever relevant subject of liberty or death—on the theory that this era of victory is no time to forget the sacrifices victory requires.

Others chose to observe the Fourth in their own way. Rushing out to celebrate the latest license confirmed by the Supreme Court of the United States, Little Rock's Say McIntosh—libertarian, American and character—arrived at the state Capitol last year with a flag for burning. "The Supreme Court justices said I can burn this flag," he explained. "This flag has never lived up to what it said." Say McIntosh doesn't understand. Like the Declaration of Independence, the flag is not only a statement of what was, but of what shall be. It is not some boastful version of the past; it is and always has been a promise for the future. O Say, can't you see? It is *we* who have not lived up to the flag.

Every July the Fourth, Americans should be reminded that the American experiment has just begun, and a new birth of freedom awaits. Just as John Adams wrote Patrick Henry in 1776: "The dons, the bashaws, the grandees, the patricians, the sachems, the nabobs, call them by what names you please, sigh and groan and fret, and sometimes stamp and foam and curse, but all in vain. The decree is gone forth..." It goes forth still, two centuries later.

Dour old John Adams, carried away for perhaps the only time in his long and responsible life, sat down to write Mrs. Adams after the decision was made to declare independence—a decision he knew would mean more bloodshed and destruction, and perhaps his personal ruination as well. Yet he assured Abigail that, "through all the gloom, I can see the rays of ravishing light and glory. I can see that the end is worth all the means, and that posterity will triumph..." Typically American, he looked to the future, and resolved to fulfill the dream. May we serve posterity as well as he and his generation served us.

VII | BASEBALL AS METAPHOR

Baseball as America

It is good that baseball cuts so deep, lest we grow too fond of it. It is America's own opera—full of slow passages and dramatic endings. It is timeless ritual and statistical precision, liberal art and exact science, finely complex and essentially simple. A field of dreams.

No wonder baseball has inspired so much bad prose and worse attempts at poetry. Nothing written about baseball can match the game itself. Each season leaves the fan with its own beneficence—or heartbreak. Some years it brings triumph and others, especially if you're a Red Sox fan, tragedy as inevitable as any in Shakespeare or the Greek classics.

Like every great recurrent enterprise, baseball is always the same and always different. The 1990 season left fans smiling, even if the smiles in Oakland seemed a bit rueful. How are the mighty fallen! The Cincinnati Reds had given Everyman an early Christmas gift: Hope, antidote to despair, fruit of uncertainty.

To quote Joaquin Andujar, late of the St. Louis Cardinals: "You can sum up baseball in one word: You never know." Sr. Andujar may have had his failings as a pitcher; his English was less than perfect; and his arithmetic may have left a couple of integers to be desired. But he had the soul of a poet. On the strength of that one observation, he ranks

185

up there with Yogi Berra, Casey Stengel and other seers of the game. (Or maybe it's down there.)

In his beautiful little book about baseball, George Will says the game is about excellence and, like the rest of us, he cannot resist using it as a metaphor: "I believe that America's real problem is individual under-stretch, a tendency of Americans to demand too little of themselves, at their lathes, their desks, their computer terminals.... I will not belabor the point but I do assert it. If Americans made goods and services the way Ripken makes double plays, Gwynn makes hits, Hershiser makes pitches and La Russa makes decisions, you would hear no more about the nation's trajectory having passed its apogee."

No, no, no. As can happen on rare occasion, Brother Will has missed in the most elegant way. He has swung wide at a high inside pitch, and is left spraddled at the end of his roundhouse sentence. His praise of Maestro La Russa must resound a trifle ironic in joyless Oakland in light of the Reds' victory over the Athletics in the '90 Series. But the big problem with his scholarly opinionation is his view of baseball as production, of art as but science in the making. It is a view of baseball as competition rather than sport, industrial rather than pastoral, individual rather than whole. It omits the Joaquin Andujars and Babe Hermans, the minor leagues and crowd noise. It skips over the game's remarkable tolerance for the mediocre, its ability to wait patiently for that one golden moment when a Cookie Lavagetto achieves immortality and is never heard from again. Can science be but art in the making?

Baseball, with all its checks and balances, is the aesthetic and spiritual equivalent of the American Constitution. It is not meant for gods, or even the ceaselessly proficient, but for fallible humans, particularly those of the American persuasion. Its base paths are wide but defined, its rules the source of endless arcane disputations but rules nevertheless. Whether one is a conservative and always roots for the team in the field, or a liberal and cheers the side at bat, in the end it is the game that counts and not how it is played.

Literary champions of baseball like Mr. Will do a great service by railing against abominations like the aluminum bat; the very sound of the game is important, and so is the ability to compare batters from age to age. Major changes in technology should be left to tennis and other encounters of the vicious kind.

The other day, a foreign exchange student at the local high school asked what he should study in order to understand America. I suggested the War Between the States and baseball. One is the rock from which we are hewn, the other a paradigm for the system, formal and informal, that imposes order while assuring the unpredictable.

Baseball must stir us yet leave behind enough peace to last through wintry times—like the Constitution itself. It must change but remain the same, avoiding sudden improvisations like the Dred Scott decision and the designated hitter, however beneficial they're said to be when first introduced. Yet it must leave room for revolutionary changes that make the game great: Brown v. Board of Education and the force-out.

Not strength but judgment is the key to baseball—not excellence but tolerance. It is a game for life, not perfection. Its stars shine brightest in a constellation. *E Pluribus Unum.* From out of many, one infield.

In baseball as in the structure of a society, it is not the goal but the pursuit that must be protected from those who would "improve" the game by destroying its essential character and unity. The players *and* the fans *and* the memory of past seasons *and* the prospects of those to come must all be fused into one whole. There must be room for Ted Williams *and* Joe DiMaggio, the New York Yankees of '27 *and* the St. Louis Browns, the driven *and* the aimless.

When baseball ceases to be symphonic, or timeless, or unifying, it will have ceased to be baseball no matter what it's called. When it is no longer closed to anarchy yet open to all and their possibilities, it will no longer be baseball, any more than America will be America.

You should be able to sum up both the nation and its pastime in one word: You never know.

The Rites of Spring

ST. PETERSBURG, Florida—Spring came here a day early. That's when the Mets and Yankees played their annual exhibition game at Al Lang Stadium, a little green jewel of a field set next to the bay. It long has been known that baseball has the power to overrule ordinary time. Minutes and hours stop when you enter a baseball stadium; they're replaced by the open-ended time of outs and innings.

Today's game has overruled the calendar, pushing the season up a day. The scoreboard says it is 1:17 in the afternoon and the temperature is 70 degrees. Under a serene blue sky, the Mets are resplendent in their home team uniforms as they take batting practice. The Yanks watch in dignified gray. The stands are almost full an hour before the game; hot dogs, beer, and baseball talk are available. Lo, the winter has gone, the rains are past, and the players are doing wind sprints in the outfield. It is undeniably spring.

The best time to come to a baseball game is early. Then your attention isn't bombarded all at once by the green, green field below, the clean dirt of the infield, the ballplayers so near, the scorecard and other refreshments in your hands while you're trying to locate your seat and find out who's up. Early arrivals can absorb one thing at a time. The knowledge that time no longer matters can be discovered and savored. It's a bit like boarding a train for a long journey. It takes a while to get settled in, and to realize that the world won't resume till you've reached the destination. Getting to a ball game on time is like arriving at the opera after the overture. The full effect requires that the preliminaries be observed.

Some fans search for the stars. ("There's Yogi!") The young players trying out are more eager, and more interesting to watch. Like the prospect of being hanged, the possibility of being consigned to the minors wonderfully concentrates the mind. It quickens not only thought but reflexes.

The grounds crew appears, easing tension. The earth is tamped down, the playing field hosed, and straight paths restored for the game's sake. It is time to meditate before the actual rites begin. The organ music starts. It is almost time.

Somewhere, perhaps only in someone's mind, there exists the perfect baseball game. Just before the opening pitch, each game holds out the possibility of perfection, the way spring does for the year. Just as Goethe theorized that somewhere there was an *ur*-pflanze from which all plants are descended, baseball is America's *ur*-game. It is the neat Platonic idealization of the system, blending individualism and team effort, talk and action, commonplace routine and high drama, a narrow focus and expanses of time and place.

The game is a return to a pastoral world of green fields and blue skies. Each spring, it seems to require more patience for Americans to settle into the baseball season and recapture its promise. The brutalities of football and the razzle-dazzle pace of basketball now compete with baseball, crowding it into a seasonal corner. Who has time for baseball any more? The game is not suited for television; the camera forecloses the watcher's vision and puts blinders on the fan. And if something isn't suitable for television, how suitable can it be for mod America?

Baseball acquires some of the fascination of a relic, and Americans come to venerate the game more than they watch it. To go to a baseball game nowadays is to cast a vote for the past and against the pressurized present. It is an act of slow, leisurely, premeditated defiance against the trim new gods of the quick and efficient. It is dense with old-fashioned, mechanical mathematics. It is a game of the long haul, of averages, of the kind of competence that only time and repetition can truly test. It is a game of watchful waiting, of patience. And it's played every day, not just weekends. Men may recall football games the way they do wars; they recall baseball games the way they do their first love. Baseball is never without the admixture of nostalgia. It offers the grace and timelessness of a dream, and exhibition baseball is the dream before the dream.

Down on the field, the teams have sent the timeless clock into motion. The Mets look like champs, the Yankees like ringers. It soon becomes apparent that these aren't the New York but the Florida Yankees, a team beset by injuries and put together out of survivors and stand-ins.

The Mets have Gary Carter catching (and hitting two for three), Wally Backman at second, and out in right Darryl Strawberry, who moves within a kind of magnetic field that attracts every eye. Carter and Strawberry hit back-to-back homers in the Mets' big inning, the third. "That one was hit so high," someone in back of me says, "it had snow on it when it came down." Another ritual incantation observed.

It was a far from perfect game in this perfect little park, but it was a perfect way to welcome spring. While walking back into the world of time and schedules, it occurs that something is missing. It's hard to say just what. It's what's missing in much of Florida's touristland facade—the saving touch of the ordinary, the feeling of hardscrabble reality that coats minor-league ball in imperfectly lighted parks, the sense of elevation on walking out into a buggy night to drive home after having watched grace triumph once again over slightly rickety environs.

It is still light after the game, and that's unnatural to anybody brought up watching the Shreveport Sports or any other minor-league ball team. This is like leaving a pleasure-dome, not a ballpark. Something gritty and real is missing. The peanuts here come already shelled in little plastic bags. I miss Ray Winder Field in Little Rock and the Arkansas Travelers. When did you say the Travs open their season?

Gone with the Red Sox

Preserving a tradition that goes back to 1918, the Boston Red Sox once again have managed to snatch defeat from the jaws of victory. It isn't getting any easier. In 1986 it looked almost impossible. But the Bosox did it, though it took seven games and some of the most improbable sequences this side of a Dickens novel. And at the end, though some thought the end would never come, the tradition was still intact: The Red Sox still had not won a World Series since 1918. In its 68th precarious year, again and again that fragile record came within an easy out of being broken.

It was a razor-close shave and an immense relief to anyone with a sense of tragedy or nobility, which often go together in baseball and other classics. Their defeat by the Mets may prove a transient disappointment in Boston, but it's also a profound assurance to note that at least one thing doesn't change in this mad, mad, Mets world. If the Mets are the team of the future, in those gaudy multi-colored *and* pin-striped uniforms, then the past, as simple and dignified as the gray uniforms of the visiting team, never looked so good.

Defeat has its consolations that victory can never know. Would the Southern character be the same without the Lost Cause? Would King Lear be a more satisfying play with a happy ending? If Dante had married his Beatrice, how long would you have given it? Would this be a better country if the new Coke had proved a success and the classic old formula had been discarded?

Victory in the modern world, it has been understood in Boston at least since Henry Adams, is undignified. It does not offer the solitude that the development of character requires. Everybody loves a winner; a loser gets to meditate in peace and quiet.

Dan Okrent, the editor of *The Ultimate Baseball Book,* says of baseball: "Most of the action exists in the mind." And tragedy is far more durable in those precincts than victory. Mr. Okrent claims that baseball is a game of "anticipation rather than experience. It's those two minutes between the action that makes baseball what it is." And Red Sox fans will soon be recollecting almost with relish not the home runs but the time the Sox had men in scoring positions with none out yet resisted all temptation, or that wondrous sixth game in 1986 when they were within one out of victory and nobody on but would not stoop, or catch, to conquer. No more than they would deign to steal bases, a form of petty larceny best left to the likes of the Mets. Baseball, like spring, is a thing not only of anticipation but of memory.

If baseball were not so American (and now Japanese) it would surely be Greek. Is there any clearer warning against hubris? Aeschylus would have been right at home in the press box and Aristophanes couldn't have found better material than the worldly, up-to-date Mets. "Baseball *is* Greek," Jacques Barzun once claimed, because it is "national, heroic, and broken up in the rivalries of city-states." Each of those polities, one might add, has its own distinctive character, style, and outfield. The Red Sox and the old Brooklyn Dodgers share a certain gallantry in defeat, but what was comic about the Dodgers is tragic in the Red Sox. It's the difference between Babe Herman and Bruce Hurst, Leo Durocher and John McNamara, Ebbets Field and Fenway Park. It was Cornelius Vermeule, curator of classical art at the Boston Museum of Fine Arts, who put Fenway Park in proper historical perspective when he called it "the Masada of sports."

What a waste if all this stoicism in defeat had been sacrificed to the mere joy of victory. What a waste of all that history, perseverance and dour acceptance. Victory would have been unnatural, like a Red Sox fan who expects the best. David Margolick captured the chronic anxiety of the Red Sox aficionado when he said that nothing less than a five-run lead could ever ease his anxiety when watching the Red Sox play—"only because Sox relievers have not figured out a way to yield a six-run homer."

Anyone with the courage to follow the Red Sox (no, it is not masochism but clear-eyed courage) knows that baseball, whatever its illusions, is not afflicted with the illusion called finality. There is always another game, another season. Like the statistics of the game, or its timeless clock, or the extent of the foul lines, baseball is infinite. Pitchers and hopes rise again in the spring—but not before a long winter is passed reflecting on opportunities unseized. After the first sharp pang of loss, there is no repining; that may be the greatest difference between chess and baseball. In baseball, there is a grand acceptance of fate. Red Sox fans, like many a veteran of middle age looking back on youth, can testify that it is better to have loved and lost than never to have lost at all. Look at what all that winning did to the character of Yankee fans, if they ever had any.

Only Yankee fans leave their team when it stops winning or the management becomes even more intolerable than usual. Those who follow outfits like the Cubs and the Red Sox have a loyalty that goes beyond the box scores and into acceptance and, finally, eternal anticipation. Some in this world wait for Godot; the luckier wait for another DiMaggio. "I like to watch college football and I can get emotional about it," Heywood Broun once wrote, "but when I want moral stimulus and confirmation for my faith in the fundamental romanticism of man I go to see professional baseball."

The State of Baseball

Roger Angell, the Montaigne of baseball writers, has decided that big-league baseball "is long past its innocent youth and well into what appears to be a disordered and destructive middle age." Many a fan might agree. A fascination with sports cars is said to be the first sign of the male menopause; just what development signaled the beginning of baseball's middle age is open to debate. Some would nominate the introduction of the designated hitter, others the pernicious influence of television. Whatever the cause, what once was an art is in danger of becoming only an entertainment.

Yet even the middle aged may be impressed by how quickly the body can bounce back from abuse. Even Mr. Angell writes of baseball's "remarkable recuperative powers." It may need them. Baseball is as much nostalgia as sport, and every season seems to produce its own threat to the game's traditions.

This was the year a long-dreaded heresy was adopted as part of the ritual when Chicago got night games at Wrigley Field, the last holdout against that practice. To treat this subject as a local zoning dispute is like referring to World War II as a difference of opinion. Some can only shudder at the thought of those ivy-covered walls and the old, hand-operated scoreboard suddenly exposed to the electric glare and arbitrary shadows of artificial light. What a fearful revolution after 72 sunlit summers.

Night baseball at Wrigley Field once seemed as unimaginable as the Cubs' winning a pennant, which hasn't happened since '45. Chicago's traditionalists long have held that the simulacrum of the sport at Comiskey Park is good enough for anybody with the poor taste to watch baseball after sunset.

When the City Council finally voted to permit this desecration at hallowed Wrigley Field, some of the more unregenerate traditionalists left chanting the ultimate threat: "Dry precinct! Dry precinct!" If the demands of television require night ball at Wrigley Field, imagine what voting the neighborhood dry would do to beer sales. That is to go too far, even in defense of tradition. Baseball without hot dogs and beer would be as unnatural as, well, as lights at Wrigley Field.

On the other hand, there are those of us who grew up watching minor-league ball under the lights. It's hard for us to imagine a more dazzling sight than the first glimpse of that bright diamond in its green setting, and the overwhelming colors of the newly painted signs shimmering across the field, transforming mere commerce into romance.

What is it that Robert Redford says in an almost offhand way at some point in the movie version of *The Natural*—"God, I love this game!" What American hasn't thought that in just those words? "God, I love this game!" It's a combination confession, prayer of thanks, and sudden realization. Such is the power of baseball over those who were captivated by it young.

To a different kind of traditionalist, ball fields don't need ivy but they must have advertisements. What is anathema to some may be ritual to others. An ivy-covered wall lacks the authenticity of an uneven row of shining new billboards for the local bottler, car dealer, cleaner's...and the inevitable sign that offers a bonus to the home-team batter who hits it.

Ivy or ads? As a matter of aesthetic judgment, it's a bit like choosing between the Hudson River School of landscape painters and Edward Hopper. What is tradition to one may seem jejune to the other.

There are other unnerving developments, as there tend to be every season. Happily, the fascination with balks seems to be fading; it needs to go the way of last season's obsession with corked bats. There is still some ominous talk about scheduling inter-league games during the season; that's the worst idea since artificial turf. The American League has become confusing enough with its 14 teams—five more than the classical number. Schedule inter-league games and that'll be the end of any hope of remembering what team belongs in what league, division, genus and species. If the good Lord had meant baseball teams to play out of their league during the season, He wouldn't have invented spring training and the World Series for that irregular purpose. Mark up one more heretical suggestion that bears the clear fingerprints of television promoters.

There have been some hopeful developments, too. Since baseball fans love new records, even at losing, the Baltimore Orioles were able to generate more interest by losing games than they did by winning them. Moral: Americans love a loser, too, at least a loser on a grand, record-setting scale.

Not since the St. Louis Browns has losing attracted so much sympathy from American fandom and so many concerned suggestions—strategic, psychological and even theological. The Browns having been the predecessor club of the Orioles, this proclivity for losing is a matter of historical continuity, a valued hallmark of American civilization.

Another good sign: Minor-league ball continues to flourish in various climes, whether the crowd is cheering the conventional Arkansas Travelers at Ray Winder Field in Little Rock or the surreal Diablos at Dudley Dome in El Paso. The final score in a Diablos game, as when El Paso beat Beaumont 35 to 21, may still have to carry a parenthetical note when it's reported: *Not a football score.* For El Paso, that's fine. Anywhere else, it would be fine but not baseball. That's an instance of another American tradition: Standards relax West of the Pecos.

How judge which developments improve the game and which don't? Just ask: Which make it more like baseball? In no other sport is the ideal picture of the game so sure a guide to actual policy. Anything that preserves the character of the game—communal, pastoral, slow-paced, ritualistic—merits encouragement. Any changes not in character are to be avoided. Beware anything that smacks of individual competitiveness, urban brashness, the hasty, or the novel.

Baseball, like any other institution, must change if it is to be preserved. But the changes should be made in the spirit of the original. Edmund Burke would understand; so would any good architect.

The Art of Gordon McLendon

He invented the Top 40 format for hit tunes, and put together 458 disparate radio stations into the old Liberty Broadcasting System in the '40s and '50s, but Gordon McLendon, "The Old Scotchman" himself, earned his place in the cherished recesses of American memory with his play-by-play radio broadcasts. Rather than the usual telegraphic account, he offered a dramatic reenactment and improvement of the game being played hundreds of miles away. Gordon McLendon didn't just report baseball games; he re-created them, complete with the crack of the bat and the roar of the crowd. You could almost smell the hot dogs. You *could* hear the peanut vendors, and the wh-u-up of a baseball sliding down the foul net. There are still fans extant who refuse to believe he wasn't on the spot, high above the stadium just behind the batter's box.

Purists were known to complain that his expertise lay not in baseball but fiction. But compare the ordinary play-by-play of those years, punctuated only by the dots and dashes of the wire, with The Old Scotchman's rendition, and ask which comes closer to capturing the heart of the game. Which is truer in that visceral sense—"ball... strike...pop out to first" or Gordon McLendon's version:

"McGurty steps up to the plate, takes a couple of good hefty swings, bends down to grab a fistful of dirt. Now he's ready. Napolski on the mound, looks back, checks the runner on second, goes into

the wind-up . . . it's a hard, high fast one, just a bit too high. Ball One.
He's been having a little trouble getting 'em low enough since the
second inning. McGurty looks to the third base coach, now he's
ready, he digs those spikes in. Napolski using a little resin now, gets
his signal, and throws—a fast one right down the middle past a
dumbstruck McGurty; the bat never left his shoulder. Strike One!
The crowd roars its approval but McGurty doesn't seem to like the
call, says something to the umpire. Manager Jack Stevens in the
dugout looks grim. The count is one and one, the visitors are down
by two in the top of the eighth, and this crowd smells a victory. Now
Napolski is ready. The batter's alert now, tugs at his cap, assumes his
stance, left foot well forward, swinging that bat menacingly, here's the
pitch, it's good, and a high, high pop up . . . it may go foul, no, it's
fair, shielding his eyes from the lights, loses it, no, he's got it! (Crowd
roars.) One out in the top of the eighth, and coming up is . . ."

The news of Gordon McLendon's death at 65 may revive the
debate over which approach comes closer to the truth of baseball. It
is the old, old tug between art and science. Although television
rendered Gordon McLendon's "art" obsolete, it has flourished
elsewhere—in politics, for example. One can trace the appeal of
Ronald Reagan's rhetoric back to the days when, as a young announc-
er, he used to broadcast detailed descriptions of Chicago Cubs games
on the basis of only the barest information over the wire. Looking
back on his career in a mellow moment, the President once explained,
and defended, how it was done:

"You'd get a little slip and it would say, 'Out, six to three.' Well,
now, Number Six on a team is the shortstop and Number Three is
first base, so you knew that had to be a ground ball to shortstop. Now,
if the game was rather dull, you could say, 'It's a hard-hit ball down
toward second base, the shortstop's going over after the ball, makes a
wild stab, picks it up, turns, and gets him out just in time!' Now I
submit to you that I told the truth. He *was* out from shortstop to first.
And I don't know whether he really ran over toward second base and
made a one-hand stab or whether he just squatted down and took the
ball when it came to him. But the truth got there and, in other words,
it can be attractively packaged."

Without getting too deeply into that age-old puzzler—"What Is Truth?"—let it be said that Mr. Reagan's working definition can have some dangerous shortcomings. At the same time, it can satisfy some powerful psychological needs—in the way that myth can be truer than fact. Some would call it falsifying; Gordon McLendon called it re-creating.

The politicians who can re-create, who can deal in myth as well as fact, may prove most in contact with their audiences, just as Gordon McLendon was more in contact with the minds of his listeners than the broadcaster who told them only, "ball...strike...pop out to first." The Old Scotchman had a hold on their fantasies, dreams, imaginations. He had a hold on the way the world should be and, who knows, may be.

By draining all color from an event, by reducing it to the bare essentials or less, have we really made it truer, or just falsified it in a different way? Contrary to the old saw, politics is the art of the seemingly *im*possible. Certainly American politics is. For what fictional account could match the history of this curious Republic?

Re-creation may be the best explanation for how the Reagan Era of stability and optimism was created (or re-created, to borrow a McLendonism) at the end of two tumultuous decades marked by a tragic war, assassinations, the virtual impeachment of a president, and a palpable loss of national confidence. Anybody who thinks politics is a science rather than an art needs to explain why political science courses are so different from politics as it actually is, the way baseball is from "ball...strike...pop out to first."

The art of Gordon McLendon may explain why Jimmy Carter—so responsible, so drab, so in charge of details—was so out of it and Ronald Reagan—so hazy on the small stuff, so inexact, so casual—was so with it. There is now even a common word for Gordon McLendon's "re-creational" style of rhetoric: anecdotal.

The dispute over the value of Gordon McLendon's art brings to mind the nature of reality:

"Balls and strikes," said the first umpire, "I calls 'em as I sees 'em."

"Balls and strikes," said the second, "I call 'em as they are."

"Balls and strikes," said the third, "they ain't nothin' till I call 'em."

There is perhaps no accounting for the mysterious tide in human affairs without considering all three views. There is certainly no explaining it without weighing the view of that third umpire, the re-creator. The Old Scotchman understood as much; so does every accomplished leader, every far-seeing visionary, every willful demagogue, and every great statesman.

Goodbye, Comiskey: The Romance of Baseball

This was the last season for good ol' Comiskey Park on Chicago's South Side—good 80-year-old Comiskey Park, to be exact. It was the oldest ballpark in the majors—older even than Fenway in Boston and Tiger Stadium in Detroit and stylish Wrigley Field on the North Side. It had to go to make room for, of course, a parking lot. The lot will serve the new, space-age Comiskey Park just across the street. It won't be the same, even if it does have natural grass and good sight lines. It won't have the memories, the history, the ghosts.

Listen to this memory: "The most wonderful time to go into Comiskey Park is early in the morning. Or late in the day, when everyone has left. You can hear the ball yard whispering, telling its stories. People will tell you it's just the wind, but I don't believe it. Babe Ruth hit home runs there. In a world that doesn't make very much sense, I like ballparks. Comiskey was like life itself."—Michael Veeck, now president of a class-A team in Pompano Beach, Fla., and son of the immortal peg-legged Bill Veeck, the last great promoter of the game.

Bill Veeck understood that baseball isn't just the national pastime but has to be something of the national circus. The peculiar dignity of baseball has to embrace the undignified, the zany, the three-men-on-third-base plays, the sight of a helicopter landing behind second base and disgorging a team of midgets dressed as Martians... No wonder they cheered that bicentennial opening day at Comiskey when Bill Veeck himself came striding out of the dugout as part of The Spirit of '76. (He was the wounded fife player with the bloodstained headband and natural limp.)

Memories. An old friend I stay in touch with recalls: "I saw my first major-league ball game at Comiskey Park. We visited Chicago cousins every summer and Cousin Dave took us. They lived in a fourth-floor walk-up on the South Side off Lawndale Avenue; I remember that we'd have to wait supper till he got in from the tavern down the block, that he ate in his undershirt—the old sleeveless kind—and that he took us to Comiskey Park. All those were new and impressive phenomena to a 10-year-old from Shreveport, La. I had never heard the word 'tavern' before—only bar—and it took me a while to figure it out. And at home only little kids got to wear underwear to the table. But most impressive of all was the ball game. On the field were players I'd only read about—like Luke Appling at short. Second base was always my favorite position, maybe because I never had the grace to play it. They always put me at third in pick-up games: good arm and not enough sense to get out of the way of a line drive.

"Anyway, I'll never forget that afternoon at Comiskey. It was a day game, of course. Weren't almost all of them then? Oh, the noise and confusion and hot dogs, and the smell and the gritty South Side air. Wondrous. How grown-up. The real world at last. It sure beat hell out of the aquarium and the museums, even the Museum of Science and Industry with its real live coal mine. And the colors. For some reason I had thought big-time baseball was played only in black-and-white—probably because of all those grainy halftones on the old sports pages. Oh, the green of the infield grass. The brightness of everything. The neat insignia of the Sox with the O and the X inside the S. But the one figure I kept staring at was the only one down there not in uniform. A thin old guy in a blue-serge suit with white hair who always held a score card in front of him, sometimes at odd angles. The visiting team was the Philadelphia A's and that was Connie Mack, Cornelius McGillycuddy himself. I think the A's won both halves of the double-header; the Sox weren't much between 1919 (the Black Sox scandal) and 1957, when Al Lopez brought 'em back to life. But Comiskey Park was something, especially that afternoon with Cousin Dave. Never will forget it.

"Now they're tearing the place down. Afraid if they don't, Tampa-St. Pete or some other Standard Metropolitan Statistical Area will steal the team. But moving across the street will be almost traumatic. The new stadium will have sky boxes. Air-conditioned, no doubt. Piped-in crowd noise. Martinis and canapes. You might as well be watching the Cubbies. Watching a baseball game from a sky box is like making love in pajamas. Sky boxes belong with the designated hitter and league expansions. Why couldn't they keep baseball down to two major leagues with eight teams apiece—the way God intended?"

My old friend expected no answer. His wasn't so much a question as the familiar cry of pain from a past remembered as golden to a present that seems sounding brass—and to a future that promises to be ever more sanitized and flavorless. Will that future have any room for memory or desire or anything but efficiency? Will anybody in neo-Comiskey Park raise the eloquent banner that was such a hit at old Comiskey? ("YUPPIE SCUM GO BACK TO WRIGLEY.") Will the new field even have bleachers worthy of the name? Will it be worthy of the South Side? That is, will it still have a saving touch of the sordid, of the Divine Comedy that is baseball? (Dante Alighieri, it should be remembered, didn't write in classical Latin but vulgar Italian. He definitely would've been a Sox fan.)

And will you still be able to smell the stockyards at the new, spiffy Comiskey Park? (Old Man Comiskey's favorite line, much practiced at the usual civic dinners, went: "As you know, we lost 102 games last year, and we've been getting a lot of complaints from the stockyards about the strong odor coming from Comiskey Park.") Far from upholding their grand and slightly aromatic tradition, will the shiny new Sox in their shiny new stadium even be aware of it?

The infield at Comiskey Park, it needs to be remembered, was built over a dump, and remained true to its foundation. William Nack, in *Sports Illustrated*, quotes Luke Appling himself on the archaeology of the place: "One day I pulled a big blue-and-white coffee pot up out of the infield. My spikes were clicking on it. They had to hold up the game and bring out three or four shovelfuls of dirt to cover up the hole. Another time I slid into home plate, and the neck of a Coca-Cola bottle cut me on the leg. That stuff had just worked its way up." Like the White Sox themselves in recent years. If they were only in the Eastern Division, they might be leading the league. Instead, they have the misfortune of being lumped with the Oakland A's, the Yankees of this era. O the times, O the mores. They don't change in baseball, or in life; they just switch franchises.

Is it baseball that has aged or only my friend? A little of both, one suspects. A lot of both, probably. But baseball cannot escape its share of the responsibility—not with its designated hitters and sky boxes. The platoon system already has been introduced on the mound; who expects a starter to go nine innings any more? Pitchers now come in at least three categories: starters, set-up men, and stoppers, one for each phase of the game. And high-tech bats, too—as if they were tennis rackets.

Soon they'll be taking the clock to the game—the way they do to football and basketball—and the essence of baseball will be gone: its pastoral timeliness, its natural pace. Look at what already has been lost. Compare Kenesaw Mountain Landis to A. Bartlett Giamatti. There you have the progression of baseball over the past half-century or so: from art to art appreciation, judgment to administration, writer to literary man. It's like comparing anything original to a self-conscious imitation, the real experience to a bad poem about it.

If there's hope, as George Orwell wrote in *1984*, it lies with the proles. That is, with the South Siders. They'll be serving sushi at Wrigley Field any day now if they haven't started already. If there's hope for baseball, it lies with the minors. The best chance of escaping the coming Sky Box Era may be found in homey little ballparks like Ray Winder Field in Little Rock, where you can still see Captain Dynamite blow himself up at second base between halves of a double-header. Bill Veeck would have understood. I miss the old Comiskey Park. But, who knows, right behind the storied ghost is a new house of dreams. It waits to be filled with the stuff of legend, and to be seen as it should be: through the eyes of a 10-year-old.